A CELEBRATION OF DISCIPLE-MAKING

D1511009

E.P.B.C. LIBRARY
Peterborough, Ontario

A
CELEBRATION
OF DISCIPLE-
MAKING

Ron Kincaid

While this book is intended for the reader's personal enjoyment and profit, it is also intended for group study. A leader's guide with Reproducible Response Sheets is available from your local bookstore or from the publisher.

VICTOR BOOKS ®
A DIVISION OF SCRIPTURE PRESS PUBLICATIONS INC.
USA CANADA ENGLAND

E.P.B.C. LIBRARY
Peterborough, Ontario

All Scripture quotations are from the *Holy Bible, New International Version,* © 1973, 1978, 1984, International Bible Society. Used by permission of Zondervan Bible Publishers.

Library of Congress Cataloging-in-Publication Data

Kincaid, Ron.
    A celebration of disciple-making / Ron Kincaid.
      p.   cm.
    Includes biographical references.
    ISBN 0-89693-793-3
    1. Evangelistic work.   I. Title
    BV3790.K52 1990   89-77637
    269'.2—dc20   CIP

---

1 2 3 4 5 6 7 8 9 10 Printing/Year 94 93 92 91 90

© 1990 by SP Publications, Inc. All rights reserved. Printed in the United States of America.

No part of this book may be used or reproduced in any manner whatsoever without written permission except in the case of brief excerpts in critical articles and reviews. For information address Victor Books, Wheaton, Illinois 60187.

CONTENTS

ACKNOWLEDGMENTS

I am indebted to many people for the writing of this book. I thank my parents who led me to Jesus Christ and nurtured me in the Christian faith. I am very grateful to my friend, Mike Donahue, a journalist, who discussed many of the ideas for this book with me and offered numerous editorial suggestions for the manuscript. Many thanks to Julie Towne, Marianne Williams and Jim Westfall who each edited several chapters for me in different stages of the development of this work. I appreciate the elders of Sunset Presbyterian Church who made possible a sabbatical leave on which I wrote this book. I thank my five boys, Tad, David, Luke, Joel and Mark who allowed me to use illustrations about them and waited patiently for me to finish portions of chapters before joining them on the tennis or basketball court.

Most of all I thank my wife, Jorie, who is my lifetime prayer and disciple-making partner. I know no one who models the principles in this book better than she.

To my wife, Jorie,
who joins me in the joy
of making disciples
and is one of the finest disciple-makers
I have ever met.

INTRODUCTION

"Hello Patrick. Hi Lisa. Please come in. Are you two more in love than you were last time I saw you?" I playfully asked. "How are you doing on your wedding plans? Are you all set for the big day?"

This was the fifth and final session I was to have with a young couple who had wandered into our church several months earlier looking for a place to be married. In our first meeting I discovered that neither of them were churchgoers. Except for rare occasions neither had attended any church in their twenty-some years. They knew next to nothing about the Christian faith. I asked them if they would be willing to attend our church as often as possible during the six-month period prior to their wedding. They agreed and seemed to enjoy the worship services and new friends they were meeting. Their homework assignment for this counseling appointment was to view Campus Crusade's video from the Gospel of Luke, *Jesus,* and to read the Gospels of Luke and John. Each time they read they were to ask the questions, "Who are you Jesus?" and "What do you want me to do?" and to write down any questions they had.

"Did you finish your homework assignment?" I queried. They had. "Do you have any questions?" I continued. Lisa pulled out a page of questions longer than my grocery list.

"How do we know the events in these stories actually happened?" she asked. They fired question after question: "Why did Jesus die on the Cross?" "Is Christianity a better approach to God than other religions?" "What is the difference between the Old and the New Testament?" "If God is good why does He allow so many people to suffer and die?"

For more than an hour I prayed that God would give me the right responses to their objections. It seemed to me that my answers were hopelessly inadequate. When we had discussed most of their questions and I had shared with them the biblical message of God's love and forgiveness through Christ, I asked them point-blank: "Where are you with Christ? Would you like to commit your lives and your marriage to Jesus?"

Catching me by surprise, they both nodded their heads and affirmed that they would like to become Christians. I had assumed that their questions were expressions of antagonism toward God's Word. Instead, they were requests of clarification to clear away the final obstacles to their faith. God was drawing them to Himself as they read the Bible, attended worship, and met numerous church members. The three of us held hands while Patrick and Lisa invited Christ to come into their lives. They committed themselves to making Christ the Lord of their marriage. After their wedding and honeymoon, Patrick and Lisa attended our new members' class and I had the privilege of baptizing them in a Sunday morning worship service.

What a thrill it was to have a part in seeing these two come to Christ. I know of no greater highlight in the ministry than seeing men and women transformed by saving faith in Christ. There are times, quite honestly, when I have wondered if pastoral work is worth all the effort. I praise God that our church has grown rapidly the past eight years. The increased numbers of people, however, have led to an expanded workload. Growth means more troubled people who need counseling appointments, more sick people to visit in hospitals, more weddings and funerals to perform, more staff to hire, more conflicts with staff to resolve, more decisions to make and meetings to attend, more problems to solve, and more facilities to build. The greater number of people a church has, the more difficult it becomes to please everyone. At times when I am rising early and staying up late to meet all the ministry demands, yet people are critical of decisions or programs, I question if my energies are well-spent. I think to myself, "Why bother? No one cares how hard I am working anyway." Then I receive a phone call from someone who says, "Ron, I need to talk to you. Your message on Sunday made me realize I need to make a change in my life. I want you to tell me how I can begin a relationship with Christ." Seeing people find Christ makes all the struggles worthwhile.

Year after year, God has blessed Sunset Presbyterian Church with the joy of seeing one or more people come to Christ each week. We have never strayed from our stated purpose—to make disciples. Keeping my focus and the church's direction on winning people to Christ has kept me on the cutting edge and our church alive with adventure. Obeying Christ's command to make disciples enables Christians to mature in their faith and churches to be vibrant and growing.

If you want to grow in your faith and see your church come alive with enthusiasm, this book is for you. Part One deals with reasons you should commit yourself to making disciples. Part Two identifies strategies for making disciples. I am convinced that a commitment to disciple-making is vital to a growing walk with Christ. Churches that want to grow must have a firm resolve to making disciples. We all know people like Patrick and Lisa, persons who need the change only Christ can effect in their lives. This volume is to aid you and your church in the process of learning to share the Good News of Christ with such people.

PART ONE

The Motive:
Why Become Involved
In the Process of Making Disciples?

CHAPTER ONE
Growing toward Spiritual Maturity

The Brooklyn Dodgers had just beaten the New York Giants for the pennant when the Giants' manager boasted to Charley Dressen, manager of the Dodgers, "You just wait till next year. Your boys will be a year older." Dressen retorted, "And what will yours be?" The New York manager haughtily replied, "Oh, ours will just be more mature."

The anecdote offers a nice distinction in words. In a year, if we're still alive, we'll all be a year older. We can't do anything about that. But will we be more mature? That's another matter, a matter about which we can do something.

In Colossians 1:28, the Apostle Paul writes, "We proclaim Him, admonishing and teaching everyone with all wisdom, so that we may present everyone perfect in Christ." The goal of the Christian ministry is to enable people to become mature in Christ. Are you progressing toward maturity in Christ? Or have you stopped growing? Ask yourself if you have the marks of maturity: the determination to obey God at any cost, the ability to feed yourself without relying on others to feed you, and the willingness to serve others.

A lot of Christians are like the boy who grows to 6'10" tall by the age of thirteen. You can't expect that youngster to take a basketball and play with coordination or finesse on the court. The boy has the height, but he doesn't have the maturity.

Similarly, many believers have grown to adulthood physically, but they are in the infant stage of their spiritual growth. They have the tools, but not the maturity to fulfill their goals in Christ. God calls all Christians to progress toward maturity in Christ.

The Problem of Christian Immaturity

One wonders how successful we have been in recent years in bringing people to Christian maturity. After his poll revealed that eight out of ten Americans consider themselves Christians, pollster George Gallup Jr. concluded: "It is a great paradox that religion is showing clear signs of revival even as the country is ridden with rising crime and other problems regarded as anti-ethical behavior to religious piety. We find there is very little difference in ethical behavior between church goers and those who are not active religiously."[1]

Gallup and others have further responded to these statistics with words to this effect: "Never before in the history of the United States has the Gospel of Jesus Christ made such inroads while at the same time made so little difference in how people live."[2] If Christians are not making a difference in society, one questions if believers are actually growing toward Christian maturity.

Since many churches are growing, Christians can be deluded into thinking that the church is making great gains in the world. In fact, the opposite is true. In his book, *The Gravedigger Files,* Os Guinness argues that though many churches are robust, bulging with people, little impact is being felt in society at large. He suggests this is because Christians are becoming secularized in their religion. Their faith is being acted out only in the private realm where it has little effect on public policy.[3] In other words, much activity occurs in churches and Christian organizations, but there is little impact on the world.

Every week I meet Christian men and women who are

struggling to grow spiritually. Though they may be church members, attend worship services, and read their Bibles and pray regularly, they feel they have reached a plateau in their Christian growth. The initial excitement they felt in coming to Christ is gone. Joy and vibrancy in the Lord seem strangely elusive. Close communion with the Lord is a sporadic experience at best. Something is missing, and it is sad.

These concerns have given birth to this book. I believe many Christians fail to grow to maturity because they have not responded in any significant way to Christ's command to make disciples. A disciple is someone who learns from Christ and is following Christ. Christ's call to make disciples is an invitation to every believer to reach out to others, so that they might choose to follow Him too. The disciple-making process includes: loving people, sharing the Good News of Jesus Christ with them, encouraging friends to become responsible church members, nurturing new believers in the Scriptures, and inviting people to become fellow workers in the disciple-making task.

Somehow we've been led astray, thinking we can grow toward maturity in Christ simply by listening to sermons or attending Bible studies, without also involving ourselves in the process of making disciples. We must come to grips with the truth that God's finest instruction comes through on-the-job training. His richest rewards are reserved for those who spend their lives in service to others—in the process of making disciples.

Three Priorities in Balance

God has called His church to pursue a balance between three great priorities: *worship, nurture,* and *outreach,* as shown in the following diagram.

In worship, we assemble ourselves together corporately to celebrate God. Nurture includes all activities that build up men and women in the faith: teaching, studying the Bible, praying,

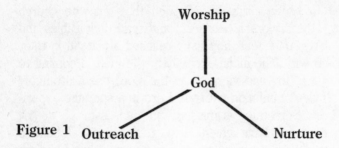

Figure 1

fellowshiping with other believers, and caring for others. Outreach encompasses our efforts to reach unbelieving, unchurched, or needy people, bringing them into Christ's church.

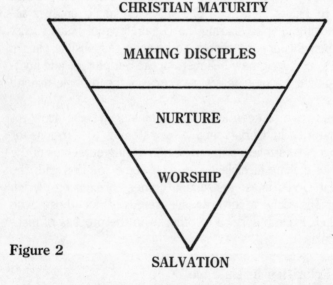

Figure 2

Notice that God must be at the center of all these pusuits. The greatest commandment is to love God with our whole heart. We love God when we praise Him, sing to Him, and are regular in our worship attendance. We also show love for God by nurturing His people. John says, "Anyone who does not love his brother, whom he has seen, cannot love God, whom he has not seen" (1 John 4:20). And love for God is shown by reaching out to His lost children in the world.

All three of these priorities—worship, nurture, and outreach—must be pursued in balance if we are to grow in Christian maturity. Figure 2 illustrates the same need for balance by showing that we grow from salvation toward Christian maturity by committing ourselves to worship, nurture, and outreach.

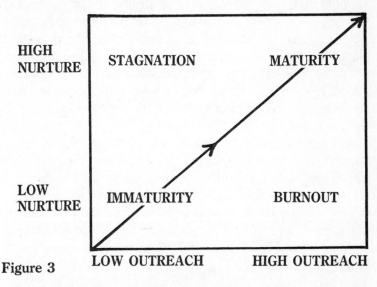

Figure 3

Some Christians believe that the only way to grow more mature in Christ is through in-depth Bible studies and heightened experiences of worship. Figure 3 illustrates the relationship between worship/nurture and outreach in the process of growing toward Christian maturity. If we focus on worship, fellowship groups, and Bible studies at the expense of reaching out to the world with God's love, then we experience spiritual stagnation. On the other hand, outreach should not be promoted as the key to Christian growth to the neglect of nurture in worship, in Scriptures, and in fellowship groups. The person who reaches out to nonbelievers without the necessary undergirding nurture will soon experience burnout. We need to hold nurture and outreach in balance if we are to grow toward Christian maturity.

I am concerned about these issues because I believe that most churches are weakest in the priority of outreach. When I surveyed the four Sunday morning worship services in our own church recently, all agreed we could improve most in the area of outreach. I found that to be significant, for we emphasize outreach at Sunset Presbyterian. I began to wonder what would happen in a church where it is not a priority in the first place? Most Christians feel the greatest deficiency in the area of outreach. Reaching out to nonbelievers is a low priority for most Christians. Yet if we do not heed Christ's call to make disciples, we deprive ourselves of the opportunity to grow toward Christian maturity.

When we commit to making disciples, we are instantly spurred on to growth in our spiritual pilgrimage. God designed life so that spiritual growth would come as an outgrowth of service to Him. If we do not give ourselves in service to others, we reach a point of stagnation. If we do not volunteer our spiritual gifts to God, they atrophy and we do not grow in our understanding of Him. But when we give ourselves to helping others come to or grow in Christ, we are delighted and surprised to see ourselves growing as well. Most Sunday School teachers or small group leaders will testify that in the process of ministering they grew more than any of their students or group members.

Every parent understands this principle. Who hasn't heard someone say, "When I became a parent I began to grow up." Why? Suddenly a parent's focus can no longer be on self. Most of the time goes into caring for his or her child. Spiritual growth occurs in the same way. The best way to grow spiritually is to become a father or mother in the Lord. As you bring someone else to Christ's church, or nurture them in the Lord, your focus is no longer on self. You might find your prayer life developing as you seek wisdom to counsel this new Christian. Most likely, you will study more to answer his or her questions. You will probably keep a careful watch on your life to set a good example to the one you are helping. I have yet to meet a Christian committed to making disciples and serving others who is not growing in faith and love for Christ.

This principle of spiritual growth is similar to that of biological cell division. Dr. Daniel Mazia, professor of zoology at the University of California at Berkeley, said, "Double or nothing. With few exceptions a living cell either reproduces or it dies: the principle is so simple that no one has bothered to call it a principle. A cell is born in the division of a parent cell. It then doubles in every respect: in every part, in every kind of molecule, even in the amount of water it contains."[4] What is true in the biological sphere is true in the spiritual realm. We either reproduce or die. We commit ourselves to making disciples and spend ourselves in service to others, or we cease to grow toward Christian maturity.

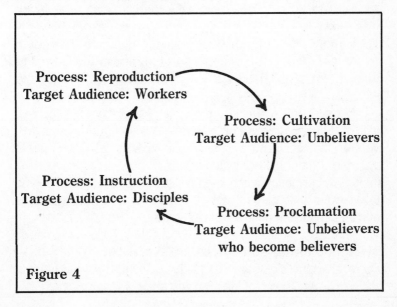

Process: Reproduction
Target Audience: Workers

Process: Cultivation
Target Audience: Unbelievers

Process: Instruction
Target Audience: Disciples

Process: Proclamation
Target Audience: Unbelievers
who become believers

Figure 4

Four Elements in the Disciple-Making Process

What does it mean to involve ourselves in the process of making disciples? There are four essential elements to disciple-making: cultivation, proclamation, instruction, and reproduction. It is most helpful to think of these four elements as an ongoing circular process as shown in figure 4 on page 21.

We are most successful in making disciples when involved in all four elements of the disciple-making circle. Nevertheless, a Christian helps Christ's church make disciples even when contributing to only one of the four parts of the process. *Cultivation* is the process of building relationships with unbelievers or those who are unchurched. *Proclamation* is presenting the Good News of Christ to an individual with the request for a response. If the presentation is clear, and the person is ready to receive the message, a disciple is born. *Instruction* must then be given to the new believer so that nurture through the Scriptures may take place.

Too often the disciple-making process stops at this point. We fail, however, if we do not take the Christian believer on to the next step in discipleship—reproduction. *Reproduction* is the point at which the Christian seeks to duplicate the faith in the lives of others. It is commitment to proclaim the Gospel to others in Word and deed in the hopes of bringing them into the church.

Reproduction is the stage when a Christian begins real growth. Laboring in the Lord's work quickens the rate of growth toward Christian maturity. Failure to understand this principle has caused thousands of well-meaning Christians to be locked in spiritual stagnation. Having lost their growing edge, they become lukewarm in their faith. Scripture teaches that disciple-making is intimately connected to Christian maturity.

Disciple-Making and Christian Maturity

There are four significant ways that making disciples helps a believer grow toward Christian maturity. First, *disciple-mak-*

ing brings the Christian a heightened experience of Christ's presence. Matthew 28:18-20 records for us some of Jesus' final words: "All authority in heaven and on earth has been given to Me. Therefore go and make disciples of all nations, baptizing them in the name of the Father and of the Son and of the Holy Spirit, and teaching them to obey everything I have commanded you. And surely I will be with you always, to the very end of the age." Jesus promises to be with us always. To whom is this promise given? It is to those who "go and make disciples." If we want to know more of Christ's presence, we must give ourselves to the mission of making disciples. Why should churchgoers expect to experience a closeness and special communion with Christ if they are not engaged in the very task for which Jesus promises His presence?

On a number of occasions someone has said to me, "Christ seems so distant from me. How can I come to experience Him being right here with me?" My answer is: Obey Him. Take your focus off of yourself and start serving others. Take Christ to other people and you will find that He always fulfills His promises. Then you'll experience His precious presence.

Second, *disciple-making brings the Christian an increased experience of Christ's power.* In Acts 1:8, Luke records for us Jesus' final words to His disciples before His ascension: "You will receive power when the Holy Spirit comes on you; and you will be My witnesses in Jerusalem, and in all Judea and Samaria, and to the ends of the earth." Christ's power is promised to those who are witnesses. Throughout the Scriptures we find that God's power is always given for a purpose. In Acts 4:31 we read, "After they prayed, the place where they were meeting was shaken. And they were all filled with the Holy Spirit and spoke the Word of God boldly." Again, His power was given so that they might speak the Word of God with boldness. If we want to experience God's power, we need to give ourselves to the task of sharing the Good News.

I discovered this principle as a high schooler: God gives

power to those who dedicate themselves to the making of disciples. I experienced the Holy Spirit's power as I reached out to my peers, seeking to bring them to Christ. I was president of my church youth group and was very involved in Young Life, a Christian outreach to high school students. Each week I packed my blue 1960 Mercury sedan full of kids to take to the Young Life club. On Sundays I faithfully brought one or two friends to church with me. My junior year I recruited a number of classmates to go to Malibu, Young Life's summer camp in British Columbia. I'll never forget the final night of camp when the leaders asked the campers who had committed their lives to Christ that week to stand. I was overwhelmed with emotion and tears came to my eyes when I saw friends I had invited standing all over the room.

Looking back, I realize that outreach caused me to grow rapidly in my faith. I was keenly aware that many people were watching my life. I needed God's power to help me be an example to the people I was hoping to influence for Christ. I had to read my Bible so I could answer some of their questions about God.

Colossians 1:9-12 illustrates that an involvement in disciple-making spurs growth in Christ. The Apostle writes, "Since the day we heard about you, we have not stopped praying for you and asking God to fill you with the knowledge of His will through all spiritual wisdom and understanding. And we pray this in order that you may live a life worthy of the Lord and may please Him in every way: bearing fruit in every good work, growing in the knowledge of God, being strengthened with all power according to His glorious might." This Scripture passage could be diagrammed as on page 25.

Paul prays that the Colossians will be filled with the knowledge of God's will, and with His wisdom and understanding. Then he prays they will obey God, please Him, and bear fruit. The most common understanding of "bearing fruit" in Scripture is to bring people to Christ. Then as we get involved

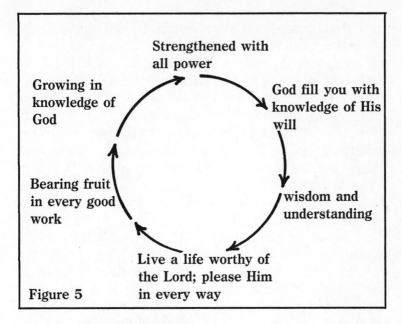

Strengthened with
all power

Growing in
knowledge of
God

God fill you with
knowledge of His
will

Bearing fruit
in every good
work

wisdom and
understanding

Live a life worthy of
the Lord; please Him
in every way

Figure 5

making disciples, Paul anticipates that we will grow further in
the knowledge of God and be strengthened with all power.
Once we give ourselves to making disciples and serving others, we grow in our faith and experience a greater measure of
Christ's power.

My wife and I want our children to grow strong in Christ
and be lifelong disciples. Since involvement in disciple-making
is a key ingredient in spiritual growth, we have invited our five
boys to join us in the process of making disciples.

Three years ago we encouraged our two oldest boys, who
were entering the first and third grades at the time, to invite a
number of their classmates to Vacation Bible School (VBS).
This task was no problem for Tad, our oldest boy. He has
enjoyed calling friends on the phone, just to talk or to invite
them to church, since kindergarten. But for David this task
presented a real challenge. He had not yet polished his telephone skills. I realize eavesdropping is not polite, but David

made the temptation almost irresistible. I overheard David call a friend and say, "Hi, can you come to Vacation Bible School with me? We'll pick you up at 8:45 A.M." He forgot to tell his friend *who* was calling, the date, or any necessary details. Sometimes when David hung up the phone, he didn't know if his friend had said, "yes," or "no!"

Together, the boys called twenty or more classmates, finally bringing thirteen kids with them to VBS. We promised to provide transportation for every child who attended. The next year our boys brought sixteen kids to VBS with them. Soon we will need a bus for transportation! Inviting friends to church activities has helped our boys grow in Christ. In the process, the boys are learning to pray for the friends they invite. Reaching out has made them aware that their friends are watching their behavior at school. They have experienced God's power firsthand during these Bible schools as they watch Him work in their friends' lives. I'll never forget their excitement, and the joy that my wife Jorie and I felt, when our boys came home from VBS announcing that several of their friends had committed their lives to Christ. Reaching out to others caused them to grow in their faith; it has always been so.

Further, *disciple-making brings the Christian a multiplied experience of Christ's joy.* Acts 2:46-47 describes the early church members who were known, above all else, for their zeal in sharing Christ: "They broke bread in their homes and ate together with glad and sincere hearts, praising God and enjoying the favor of all the people. And the Lord added to their number daily those who were being saved." They experienced genuine joy because they were seeing people come to Christ daily. They couldn't help but get excited.

After Jesus washed His disciples' feet, showing them a vivid example of a lifestyle of service, He said, "Now that you know these things, you will be blessed if you do them" (John 13:17). We are happiest when we are serving and caring for others.

Some of the most unhappy people I know are Christians who have never discovered the joy that comes from serving others. They have forgotten their purpose. Peter tells us our purpose: "But you are a chosen people, a royal priesthood, a holy nation, a people belonging to God, that you may declare the praises of Him who called you out of darkness into His wonderful light" (1 Peter 2:9). We are called to spread the news about Christ. I have observed that the more people in the church are given to gossip, backbiting, and criticism, the further they are from any significant role in making disciples. Many in the church are like caged hunting dogs. With no birds to hunt they spend their time snarling, growling, and biting at each other. However, if people are turned loose and challenged to fulfill their calling to make disciples, they soon stop bickering with each other. If we want to stop "tongue trouble" in the church, we must motivate people to participate in making disciples. The unhappiness that results from focusing on ourselves and our problems vanishes when we respond to Christ's call to make disciples. Disciple-making brings joy.

Finally, *disciple-making brings the Christian a deeper experience of Christ's promises.* A great many of Christ's promises are reserved for those who are obeying Christ's command to "go and make disciples." Many of His assurances are for those in the trenches of spiritual warfare. His promises to the persecuted presume that they are seeking to make disciples, for one is unlikely to face persecution unless speaking out for Christ. Ephesians 6:11-12 tells us, "Put on the full armor of God so that you can take your stand against the devil's schemes. For our struggle is not against flesh and blood, but against rulers, against the authorities, against the powers of this dark world and against the spiritual forces of evil in the heavenly realms." God promises spiritual armor for His people. But who needs armor but the one involved in Kingdom warfare? Warfare is risky business; it puts us out where the bullets fly; it forces us to trust and obey our commander Jesus Christ. But if we hang around the base camp, surrounded by Christians, who needs a commander?

Christ's promises mean the most to us when we're weary from battle and feel we can't go on. If we want to understand more of God's promises, we may need to step into the deep— to serve others and seek to touch them with Christ's love. Our own resources simply will not suffice; we will be forced to cling to His promises.

An involvement in disciple-making is essential to Christian maturity. Go and make disciples. Give yourselves to the church's calling to make disciples and you will be ushered into a whole new experience of Christ's presence, power, joy, and promises.

In Matthew 9:36-38 we read, "When He saw the crowds, He had compassion on them, because they were harassed and helpless, like sheep without a shepherd. Then He said to His disciples, 'The harvest is plentiful but the workers are few. Ask the Lord of the harvest, therefore, to send out workers into his harvest field.' " Jesus told us few people give themselves to making disciples. This explains why few people ever grow to Christian maturity.

Do you want to grow in Christ this year? Do you want to get out of spiritual diapers? Then commit yourself to making disciples. Disciple-making is a richly rewarding experience. Give yourselves to the process of making disciples, and you will take a giant step forward toward Christian maturity.

NOTES

1. Erwin Lutzer, "Religion A La Carte," *Moody Monthly,* July/August 1984, 65.

2. Walter A. Henrichsen, *How to Disciple Your Children* (Wheaton, Ill.: Victor Books, 1981), 105.

3. Os Guinness, *The Gravedigger Files* (Downers Grove, Ill.: InterVarsity Press, 1983), 49–91.

4. David A. Womack, *The Pyramid Principle* (Minneapolis: Bethany Fellowship, 1977), 137.

CHAPTER TWO
Gaining a Christian Perspective on Life

Wh at time is it? What time is it for those of us who live on after the tragic death of our dear friend who lost her life this week?" These were questions I asked the crowd of 400 people gathered to remember the life of an eighteen-year-old girl who died in a freak accident at the Oregon Coast.

The Oregon Coast is one of God's most beautiful creations. To watch the deep blue waters of the Pacific Ocean beat against shoreline rocks and sand is a breathtaking affair. These same elements that create beauty can also be harsh and dangerous as this young high schooler discovered. Her last earthly walk was along some logs lying in shallow water along the beach. Suddenly a huge wave rolled in and lifted a log beneath her. As the log came down, it crushed her helpless body. One moment she was jumping and laughing, the next she was lifeless and cold.

What time was it? I suggested to these horrified friends and relatives that it was a time for understanding. It was a time to understand that life is short and unpredictable. I suspected most of the people were wondering about those unspoken but often contemplated questions: "Where is she now?" "Is she spending an eternity with God or apart from God?" "Was she ready to die?"

Often it takes someone's death to bring us to a knowledge of life. Such times cause us to wonder, "What is life all about? What happens to me after I die?" Scripture teaches that life is a choosing ground. We are given the opportunity to choose to follow the will of God and spend an eternity with Him, or to follow our own self-will and spend an eternity apart from God. To come to such an understanding of life is to cultivate what we call a "Christian perspective." A Christian perspective causes us to see every person we meet through the eyes of eternity. We recognize that people either spend an eternity with Christ or without Him. This awareness should give us an urgency about sharing the news of Christ with everyone we meet.

Life's uncertainty should motivate us to spread the message of Christ. The sad truth, however, is that urgency is frequently missing. Many Christians feel little responsibility to tell others about Jesus Christ. They believe this is the pastor's job. How markedly we differ from the early church, where every believer saw his or her task as telling others about Christ.

Priorities for Many Christians

If many Christians feel little responsibility to share the message of Christ, what are their priorities? Why is the eternal perspective so often missing in our Christian worldview? Why is it that so many Christians sense no urgency to tell other people about the Gospel? I've identified six priorities in my life that hinder me from sharing the Gospel with other people. Possibly you will recognize some of them from your life. They often take precedence over the urgent matter of spreading the story of Christ. All six of these are acceptable Christian pursuits; they find biblical support and are important priorities. The danger comes as they displace the higher priority of bringing men, women, and children to an encounter with Jesus Christ.

One priority of many Christians is *acquiring material things.*

Everyone needs food, clothing, and shelter. Money is a necessity. The danger comes when our time is consumed with acquiring and caring for material possessions at the expense of concern for the eternal destiny of friends and neighbors. If young people learn by our example that comfort is the main goal, how can we anticipate that they will be any different? If we have grown to love our material possessions so that they have become more than tools to help us reach others, then they have become a snare. When I am spending too much time fixing things around the house or working in the yard, I try to remind myself that these things have no place in heaven, so I shouldn't spend too much time on them.

Another priority that can impede our pursuit of eternal matters is *the pursuit of success*. In one sense this is a noble goal. God calls us to be the best that we can be. We are to pursue excellence in all that we do. Imbalance occurs, however, if while seeking to be successful we sell out to the world's values and lose our Christian distinctiveness. In Matthew 5:13, Jesus said, "You are the salt of the earth. But if the salt loses its saltiness, how can it be made salty again? It is no longer good for anything, except to be thrown out and trampled by men." If, in order to become popular or successful, we become like the world, we have paid too high a price. If seeking to be successful in some field or activity means we have no time for God, no opportunities to point people to Christ, no time for family and friends, then the cost is too great.

Gordon MacDonald, in his book *Ordering Your Private World,* relates this story: "A close friend tells of sitting in an office with several working associates while the office manager, a woman who had worked for the company for fifteen years, made a plea for a week off to be with a sick baby. She made the mistake of responding tearfully when the boss refused her request. When he turned and saw her tears, he snarled, 'Clean out your desk and get out of here; I don't need you anyhow.' When she was gone he turned to the horrified onlookers and said, 'Let's get one thing straight; you're all here for only one reason: to make me money. And if you don't like it, get out right now!' "[1]

If the cost of success is the loss of our humanity and our eternal perspective, the price is too much to pay.

Still another priority for many of us is *the safety and security of our families*. Again, this is a legitimate concern. We have a responsibility to provide for our family's safety and security. Financial services, including insurance, is one of the most rapidly growing sectors of our modern economy. By saving and investing we prepare for retirement and for times of special need. Some parents save for years to send their children to private Christian schools. There is nothing wrong with making such choices. The problem comes when all our time, money, and efforts are expended for our families. There's a problem when nothing is left for reaching out to the lost and needy. Our greatest danger is that we will develop a "spiritual cocoon" mentality in attempting to protect ourselves and our families from evil in the world. In the process we cut ourselves off from the world Christ has called us to evangelize.

Another popular priority is *good health*. Never before in the history of the world has there been such an interest in physical fitness. I try not to overdo in this matter of fitness. I feel like the man who said, "I'd say I am pretty fit for a man of 60. First thing in the morning, I bend down and touch my slippers 50 times. Then, if I feel like it, I get out of bed and put them on." Health clubs and health food stores are doing a booming business. Good health is an important priority. Regular exercise and a nutritious diet are essential to good health. Acquiring the proper attitude is a matter of balance. In 1 Timothy 4:8, Paul says, "Physical training is of some value, but godliness has value for all things, holding promise for both the present life and the life to come." Balance is lost when we spend so much time working out, going to doctors, and focusing on our physical appearance, that no time is left to devote to evangelism.

Still another Christian priority is *the acquisition of Bible knowledge.* This is an important priority. Many of our problems are caused by a lack of biblical knowledge. You may wonder what could possibly be wrong with gaining knowledge of the Bible. The danger comes in failing to understand that the best way to learn God's truths is through serving Him. Most of what we learn about God is not picked up in classrooms or Bible studies. We learn more about Him as we obey Him and seek to involve ourselves in the process of making disciples. Nothing exasperates me more than to see Christians involved in several weekly Bible studies while having no meaningful contact with nonbelievers. They think they are growing mature in Christ, but most of our knowledge of God comes through "on-the-job" training. Your level of biblical literacy doesn't matter. If you are not living on the wavelength of Christ's Great Commission, you are destined to being irrelevant to God's purposes in the world. Read your Bible, get in a small group Bible study, but don't let these prevent you from actively serving God. Bible study is calculated to enable you to make disciples; it should never keep you from doing so.

Still another priority for Christians is *finding fellowship and making friends with other Christians.* Fellowship is essential for the growing believer. We need the prayer support, encouragement, friendship, and accountability that fellowship provides. However, when all our attention becomes focused on "our" support and "our" friendships, we become ingrown in our relationships. The priority of reaching out to others diminishes. Christians need comfort, healing, and encouragement. We must not forget, however, that the purpose of support is to strengthen us for fulfilling Christ's mandate. If all of our time is spent with believers and fellow church members, we will never have time to present the Gospel to those outside of Christ.

Time and again I have watched men and women become Christians and find their home in the church. The first days of their new Christian life they were on "fire" for Christ, were veritable "furnaces" for the Kingdom, and wanted all their friends to find Christ and come to church. Then as they develop Christian friends and get more involved within the church, I observe their flame for sharing the Gospel slowly burn down to a faint glimmer. At last, I despair to even find the "pilot light" of evangelistic concern within them. What has gone wrong? The fellowship and Christian friendships which were calculated to support them in their ministry in the world gradually displace their efforts to reach out to the world.

All six of these priorities, important as they are, must not be pursued to the exclusion of disciple-making. Unless they are sought with the goal of helping us point men and women to Christ, they become a case of good things keeping us from first things. We must not lose sight of the 3 billion people in the world who are outside of Christ.

We've looked at matters that are important to most Christians. Now, what are God's priorities? God wants to meet His people's material needs. He wants us to excel in everything. He wants us to be safe and secure. He wants us to have good health and graciously heals many of our diseases. He desires that we know and study His Word. He instructs us to seek Christian fellowship and to encourage one another. Nevertheless, His overriding concern is that His lost children be found. We read in 2 Peter 3:9, "The Lord is not slow in keeping His promise, as some understand slowness. He is patient with you, not wanting anyone to perish, but everyone to come to repentance." God sent His Son to earth for this reason, so that everyone now has the opportunity to be reunited with Him. God's overriding priority is that men and women make Him their Lord and become disciples.

The Urgent Priority of Making Disciples
A Christian perspective leads believers to an urgency about making disciples. There are at least four reasons why Chris-

tians should cultivate an urgency about making disciples. First, *making disciples is an urgent priority for Jesus Christ.* Jesus told us, "The Son of Man came to seek and to save what was lost" (Luke 19:10). When Jesus called His disciples to follow Him, He said, "Come, follow Me, and I will make you fishers of men" (Matthew 4:19). Since we are called to follow in Jesus' footsteps, it becomes clear that our purpose and our priority should be His—to seek the lost as "fishers of men." Christ came on a mission to reconcile men and women to God. His quest must be our quest. His passion must burn in our hearts.

After Christ's ascension, the Holy Spirit carried on Christ's work of reaching the lost through the members of the early church. In Acts 5:42, we read, "Day after day in the temple courts and from house to house, they never stopped teaching and proclaiming the good news that Jesus is the Christ." Again, in Acts 6:7, we find, "So the Word of God spread. The number of disciples in Jerusalem increased rapidly, and a large number of priests became obedient to the faith." The early church had no mission board. There was no evangelism committee. They erected no buildings. Members simply believed Christ was the long-awaited deliverer, that He had died, risen, and was now in the place of power in the universe. Why did they share the message of Christ with such urgency? From whom did they learn the importance of making disciples? Jesus Christ was the source. Making disciples was Christ's priority, and so it was theirs. Now it must be ours.

A second reason for urgency in making disciples is that *it has been a priority for God since the beginning of time.* Some people think that making disciples is strictly a New Testament phenomenon. However, that is not the case. Throughout the Old Testament we find that God's purpose was to show the whole world that He alone was God. This was the reason He brought the plagues on the land of Egypt through the hand of Moses. We read in Exodus 7:5, "And the Egyptians will know that I am the Lord when I stretch out My hand against Egypt and bring the Israelites out of it." Again, in Exodus 9:14, God says, "This time I will send the full force of My plagues against you and against your officials and your people, so you may know that there is no one like Me in all the earth." God did not send plagues on Egypt because He loved the Israelites and hated the Egyptians. No, it was to show His power, so that people all over the earth would hear of Him and believe. In Exodus 12:38 we read, "Many other people went up with them." Many Egyptians were convinced and chose to leave the land of Egypt with the Israelites to worship the one true God.

Solomon understood that God was looking for disciples all over the world when he prayed, in 1 Kings 8:60, that God would turn Israel's heart toward Him, "so that all the peoples of the earth may know that the Lord is God and that there is no other."

When God healed Naaman, the commander of the army of the king of Aram, through the hand of Elisha, His purpose was to spread His glory to people of another country. In 2 Kings 5:15 we read, "Then Naaman and all his attendants went back to the man of God. He stood before him and said, 'Now I know that there is no God in all the world except in Israel.'"

When Hezekiah was challenged by Sennacherib, the commander of the Assyrian army, he prayed for victory, not just for his own people's safety, but so that all the world would know of the one God. In 2 Kings 19:19, Hezekiah prayed, "Now, O Lord our God, deliver us from his hand, so that all kingdoms on earth may know that You alone, O Lord, are God." He knew that God was the only God and he wanted all people on the earth to know it too.

From the beginning of time God has been seeking believers all over the world. His priority has not changed, nor should ours.

A third reason for urgency in making disciples is because *there is a need for people to hear the message of Christ.* One of

Jesus' greatest claims was recorded in John 14:6: "I am the way and the truth and the life. No one comes to the Father except through Me." If Christ spoke the truth, as we believe He did, and we care at all about other people, then we must share the message of Jesus.

The apostles believed the same truth: "Salvation is found in no one else, for there is no other name under heaven given to men by which we must be saved" (Acts 4:12). This truth motivated them to share the news of Christ. When we care about people we will do all we can to give them this message.

The Apostle Paul taught the same truth. He wrote, "For there is one God and one mediator between God and men, the man Christ Jesus" (1 Timothy 2:5). Only one way: Jesus Christ. This conviction has motivated the church to reach out since its earliest days.

C.S. Lewis in his Narnian tale, *The Silver Chair,* clearly communicates this truth in a scene where the young girl Jill meets Aslan, that massive lion who is the Lord of Narnia and the Christ figure.

"Are you not thirsty?" said the Lion.

"I'm dying of thirst," said Jill.

"Then drink," said the Lion.

"May I—could I—would you mind going away while I do?" said Jill.

The Lion answered this only by a look and a very low growl. And as Jill gazed at its motionless bulk, she realized that she might as well have asked the whole mountain to move aside for her convenience.

The delicious rippling noise of the stream was driving her nearly frantic. "Will you promise not to—do anything to me, if I do come?" said Jill.

"I make no promise," said the Lion.

Jill was so thirsty now that, without noticing it, she had come a step nearer. "Do you eat girls?" she said.

"I have swallowed up girls and boys, women and men, kings and emperors, cities and realms," said the Lion. It didn't say this as if it were boasting, nor as if it were sorry, nor as if it were angry. It just said it.

"I daren't come and drink," said Jill.

"Then you will die of thirst," said the Lion.

"Oh dear!" said Jill, coming another step nearer. "I suppose I must go and look for another stream then."

"There is no other stream," said the Lion.[2]

There is no other stream; there is no other way. That is the message we share. That is the urgency. Your friends who have not placed their trust in Jesus Christ are headed to an eternity apart from God.

You might object, "That doesn't seem right or fair." I used to wonder that myself. The seeming unfairness of there being only one way to God troubled me until I had a life-changing discussion with a young man in Thailand. My senior year at college I decided to take advantage of the travel benefits I received as the son of a United Airlines pilot. I planned a trip around the world, visiting Presbyterian missionaries in each country, to learn what God was doing. In Thailand, I made friends with a Thai college student who had recently become a Christian. I remember saying to him one day, "Grassani, what do you think of the idea of saying Jesus Christ is for Westerners and Buddha is for you?"

He whirled around and said, "Oh no, Ron. No, Buddhism is dead. It is total darkness. Don't say that. We need Jesus Christ just like you do."

Some people take exception to the claim that Jesus is the only way to God. They accuse us of being narrow-minded. Yet, is it narrow-minded to say $2 + 2 = 4$? Jesus' claim to be the one way to God is only as narrow-minded as any other truth claim.

Yet, you still might object. It doesn't seem fair for Christ to be the only way when so many people have never heard an understandable presentation of the Gospel. I share your concern, but I remind myself to trust the assurances of Scripture that God is always fair with people. Since Christ is the only way, there is a crucial need for us to share His message. The sad news, however, is that many Christians feel little responsibility to spread the Word. We have lost our urgency to tell the world about Christ. We are apathetic. Satan is winning the battle when he convinces Christians that it is narrow-minded to make exclusive truth claims. But, is it more insensitive to share that Christ is the only way, or to let a friend go off to a Christless eternity without ever hearing the Gospel?

David Barrett, in the *World Christian Encyclopedia,* tells us that of 224 million Americans, 27 million or 12 percent have no religious affiliation whatsoever. Some 36 million or 16.2 percent are Christians in name only. That means that in a survey, they may say they are Catholic, Methodist, or Presbyterian, but they do not go to church. Some 18.1 million or 8.1 percent are not practicing Christians. Another 14.6 million or 6.5 percent call themselves practicing Christians, but attend church rarely. Putting these groups together, 95.7 million Americans, or 42.8 percent, are unchurched and candidates for the Gospel.[3] These are conservative figures, because many others who are church members may call themselves practicing Christians, but in reality they are functionally unchurched. In other words, they seldom attend church. A recent Gallup survey revealed that only 26 percent of Americans attend church weekly.[4] The figures are staggering. You and I are in contact with scores of people every week who are desperately in need of Jesus Christ. They are in need, but are we willing to tell them? Or are we too busy with our other priorities?

A final reason for urgency is because *disciple-making is essential to Christian growth.* This is the truth, unknown by many, that motivates me. When we take the time to reach out and share with others what Christ has done in our lives, we always grow in our faith. When we take the step to reach out to others, God fills us with His power. The Holy Spirit we find in Scripture is always the Spirit of witness. When we offer ourselves to the Lord for the purpose of proclamation, we experience the filling of the Holy Spirit. As you give yourself in service to making disciples, you will find your faith growing immeasurably.

I was asked to lead the Young Life Club at a local high school during my junior year in college. Very few teenagers were attending the club when the year began. Several months into the year I met a senior named Steve. He was popular with his peers. Typical of many high schoolers, Steve enjoyed a lot of laughs during school hours and plenty of partying on the weekends. Then God got a grip on his life. Steve began coming to the club meetings. He gave his life to Christ. He became a regular at our weekly Bible studies and started coming to worship on Sundays. He grew rapidly in his faith, but I would not attribute his growth spurt to the club meetings, Bible studies, and worship services. The primary reason he matured in Christ was because he began to bring his drinking buddies to Christ. The same rowdy group he hung around with on Friday nights was packed into his car on Monday nights to bring to the club meetings. Singlehandedly, Steve invited and brought thirty friends to our spring weekend camp. He leaped ahead spiritually because his focus was not on himself, but on introducing others to Christ. Today, Steve is still bringing friends and high school young people to Christ. He is a member of our church and serves as the regional director for Young Life.

Take the step of faith. Give yourself to making disciples. Share your excitement about Christ with a friend. Volunteer to teach Sunday School. Invite somebody to church with you. Plan to spend time with someone who doesn't know Christ. You will experience the thrill of building a bridge between someone and God. In the process you will find yourself growing in Christian maturity.

Like that young girl who tragically lost her life at the Oregon Coast, we all will die some day. When we die, we want to live with Christ in heaven. We will want to say that we gave our lives to matters of eternal importance—seeking to usher men and women into an eternity with Christ.

NOTES

1. Gordon MacDonald, *Ordering Your Private World* (Nashville: Oliver Nelson, 1984), 35.

2. C.S. Lewis, *The Silver Chair* (Harmondsworth, Middlesex, England: Penguin Books, 1953), 26–27.

3. David Barrett, *World Christian Encyclopedia* (Oxford: Oxford University Press, 1982), 711–713.

4. Sara Rubenstein, "Christmas Services Draw Non-affiliated Christians into Churches," *Oregonian,* 25 December 1989.

CHAPTER THREE

Enabling Our Churches to Grow

There is a pattern found all too often in thousands of churches across America and around the world. A new church is started; the church grows over a period of months, or years; the church plateaus—it no longer grows in membership or in planting new churches; then the church begins to decline. But why do churches stop growing?

Many factors contribute to the growth or decline of a church. One factor that will stop a church's growth faster than any other is the loss of a consistent and continual commitment to making disciples. A church ceases to grow when the pastor or members of that church no longer want it to grow. Such a possibility may surprise you. Don't all pastors and church members want their churches to grow? Believe it or not, the answer is no.

A few years ago a nationwide survey was taken by Larry Richards. Five thousand pastors were randomly selected across denominational lines. They were asked to prioritize "the greatest needs in strengthening the life and program of your church." Richards reported what he considers a surprising result: less than half of the pastors gave high priority to "planning and implementing church growth." Rather than growth, their priorities were centered on maintenance.[1] Many pastors feel that serving and meeting the needs of their members is of higher importance than reaching the lost for Jesus Christ. Pastoring a growing church means more work, more people to care for, and more decisions to make. Many pastors are not willing to pay that price.

Evangelism is not a high priority in many churches. The Summary Report of the Committee on Membership Trends approved by the General Assembly of the United Presbyterian Church U.S.A. in 1976 revealed, "Only 54 percent of growing congregations have an organized program of membership recruitment. Few congregations report more than a moderate level of involvement by their members in recruiting new members. Rather, there is heavy reliance on the pastoral staff.[2] Only a fourth of the churches stated that they trained members for personal evangelism. No more than 10 percent of the respondents in their study rated evangelism among the three most important aspects for their church."[2]

Another survey among Presbyterian churches revealed that sharing the Gospel with the unchurched was the task receiving the lowest emphasis in Presbyterian congregations and rated as most needing greater expression. Only 1 percent of session members said that developing and supporting the gifts of laity in day-to-day mission is among the two tasks that their congregation does best.[3]

In 1965 the Presbyterian church reported 180,000 people became members by Confession of Faith—they became Christians and were baptized into the church. In 1985 the reunited Presbyterian Church U.S.A. reported only 90,000 new members by Confession of Faith.[4] We should not be surprised at this decline in number of converts. It is the direct result of less emphasis on evangelism.

I assure you, this is not a problem unique to Presbyterians. There is a natural tendency in all churches to slowly replace the Christ-given commandment, "Go and make disciples," with other priorities. I believe the greatest desire in life for many Christians is to labor fruitfully among their unchurched friends.

The sad truth, however, is that these desires are frustrated by the lack of support in their church and the lack of any training in the necessary skills. The church staff and elders must lay the track for the train. They must set the example, provide the training, and create the structure to enable the church body in the task of making disciples. Nevertheless, many church members gain little support from their church for their disciple-making work, because evangelism is no longer a primary emphasis in the church. The call to "go and make disciples" frequently is replaced by other concerns, which, no matter how noble, must still be secondary in importance.

Typical Church Priorities

What are the priorities of many churches? One priority that has replaced making disciples in some churches is *building maintenance*. The original focus may have been to go where people are to reach them with the Gospel. But as people have been won to Christ, the church must erect new buildings to house the people. Slowly, almost imperceptibly, the church's focus shifts from reaching people to maintaining and protecting "their" buildings. The buildings that were first built so that they could reach more people ironically become a hindrance to reaching them.

The Reverend T.O. Wedel writes this modern parable that expresses the propensity for all churches to become ingrown:

On a dangerous seacoast where shipwrecks often occur there was once a crude little lifesaving station. The building was just a hut, and there was only one boat. But the few devoted members kept a constant watch over the sea, and with no thought for themselves they went out, day or night, tirelessly searching for the lost. Many lives were saved by this wonderful little station, so that it became famous. Some of those who were saved and various others in surrounding areas wanted to become associated with the station and give of their time and money and effort for the support of its work. New boats were bought and new crews were trained. The little life saving station grew.

Now the life saving station became a popular gathering place for its members. Less of the members were interested in going to sea on lifesaving missions, so they hired lifeboat crews to do this work. The lifesaving motif still prevailed in the club decoration, however, and there was a liturgical life saving boat in the room where initiation took place. About this time, a large ship was wrecked off the coast, and the hired crews brought in boats loaded with cold, wet, and half-drowned people. They were dirty and sick and some had black skin and some had yellow skin. The beautiful new club was considerably messed up. So the property committee immediately had a shower house built outside the club where the victims of shipwrecks could be cleaned up before coming inside.

At the next meeting, there was a split in club membership. Most of the members wanted to stop the club's life saving activities as being unpleasant and a hindrance to the normal life of the club. Some members insisted on life saving as their primary purpose, and pointed out that they were still called a life saving station. But they were finally voted down and told that if they wanted to save the lives of all various kinds of people who were shipwrecked in those waters, they could begin their own life saving station down the coast. They did.

As the years went by, the new station experienced the same change that had occurred in the old. It evolved into a club, and yet another life saving station was founded. History continued to repeat itself, and if you visit that coast today, you will find a number of exclusive clubs along that shore. Shipwrecks are still frequent in those waters, but most of the people drown![5]

Any church that grows needs to buy property, build buildings, and purchase equipment to continue ministering. The danger lies in the focus shifting from reaching people to maintaining buildings. When that occurs, the church will cease to grow.

Another priority that can replace the call to "make disciples" is *music and the arts*. Music that was originally used as a means of reaching the lost slowly becomes an end in itself and the focal point of the church. This can happen with classical or contemporary music. You can tell if music and and arts have replaced making disciples by looking at the results. Do these activities result in disciples being born? You see, if a church has the most wonderful cathedral choir, the best band or orchestra, the most stimulating concerts, the finest dramas and plays, inspiring musicals, or the most expensive pipe organ in town, it won't matter much if these strengths do not contribute to the church-wide task of making disciples.

Another emphasis that can subtly replace the disciple-making priority is *fellowship*. We need Christian friendships, the support of other believers praying for us, and accountability to a group of people who care about us if we are to grow toward Christian maturity. The danger comes when fellowship is sought as an end in itself and it no longer has any significant relationship to the church's primary mission. You can usually tell when fellowship has taken precedence over disciple-making—the church stops growing. No new disciples are being won to Christ. The groups that were originally formed to strengthen people in their faith slowly cause people to become so satisfied and comfortable that they lose all interest in seeking to bring their friends to Christ. We begin to hear statements like, "Our group, or class, or church is just the right size. Let's not bring anybody else in." The very activity designed by God to support our discipling, eventually becomes an impediment to doing so.

A number of years ago I had the privilege of leading a man

to Christ. He quickly became a member of our church and was excited about his newly discovered faith in Christ. He told me of dozens of friends he wanted to bring to the church. Constantly, he asked others to pray for his attempts to reach out to these friends.

That was several years ago. Since then he has gotten involved in Sunday School classes and small groups in the church. He has made a lot of close friends within our church membership. A couple of months ago I asked him who he was going to invite to a special "friendship" Sunday. He replied, "Ron, I don't have any friends who aren't Christians." I couldn't believe my ears. In a few short years, he had changed from a person who had tremendous zeal for reaching people to one who could name no non-Christian friends, let alone reach out to them. Fellowship had become a more important priority for him. In the process he had lost much of his enthusiasm for the Lord. Fellowship is essential, but it must always be focused toward the further end of reaching more disciples.

Still another priority that replaces disciple-making in some churches is *education*. Once again, education is vital to the Christian life. We need to know our Bibles. We do well to be instructed in theology and the history of Christianity. However, we must understand that biblical instruction is always given to better equip for service. Learning God's truths better prepare for our mission to make disciples. One signal that education may have preempted disciple-making is when the Sunday School or church ceases to grow. Education is critical to the development of a disciple, but its goal of enabling Christians to share God's love with others must remain constant.

Other churches make *social services* their top priority. A church that is obedient to Jesus Christ must meet the physical and material needs of people. Christ called us to feed the poor, house the homeless, visit the prisoners, and heal the sick. But churches go awry when their need-meeting programs satisfy the physical but not the spiritual needs of people. In such cases, the church provides people with no more help than do agencies of their secular counterparts. Though they may be kind to people, they ultimately fail in kindness toward people by withholding what society needs most of all—the words of eternal life.

One final way the church can be led astray from its primary mission is by overinvolvement in *political action*. The church ought to show concern about political issues. We encourage Christians to run for public office, get involved in politics, and expect their faith to impact their political views.

The danger of the church becoming overinvolved in the political realm is twofold. First, it may keep us from the more important task of making disciples. The focus is on changing society rather than changing hearts. Second, it reduces church growth because it almost always leads to church conflict. When calls for political action are given from the pulpit or by a church body, it polarizes people according to their political viewpoints. The polarization leads to disunity. When a church is experiencing conflict, people are far less likely to invite friends into their fellowship. When people stop inviting people to church, the church ceases to grow. There is a place for political action in the church, but once again, it must be secondary to the primary task of making disciples.

All of these church ministries are important and have their proper place. They must be secondary, however, to God's call for His church to make disciples. They have their place only as they compliment and contribute to spreading the Good News.

God's Priorities for His Church

What are God's priorities for His church? First, *God wants His church to exhibit a balance between three biblical priorities.* The Scriptures teach us that the church shows love for God through three priorities: worship, nurture, and outreach. The healthy church will hold these three in balance. Total emphasis on outreach is no more healthy than an absorption in nurture.

In Acts 2:42-47 we see that the early church had the perfect balance of these three priorities. We read, "They devoted themselves to the apostles' teaching and to the fellowship, to the breaking of bread and to prayer. [That's nurture.] Everyone was filled with awe, and many wonders and miraculous signs were done by the apostles. [That's outreach.] All the believers were together and had everything in common. Selling their possessions and goods, they gave to anyone as he had need. [That's nurture.] Every day they continued to meet together in the temple courts. [That's worship.] They broke bread in their homes and ate together with glad and sincere hearts, [That's nurture.] praising God, [That's worship.] and enjoying the favor of all the people. And the Lord added to their number daily those who were being saved." [That's outreach.]

Worship, nurture, and outreach are all needed to bring a believer to Christian maturity. However, when the church is out of balance, one must be emphasized over the other. Like the pendulum which swings from one extreme to another to be restored to balance, the church must emphasize the area in need of strengthening. I believe the area of weakness today is outreach. Many churches have grown inward in their focus. There is a built-in propensity in all churches to turn inward. Gradually, they find more and more of their funds are spent on themselves, their facilities, and their members. The priority of looking outward to make disciples must be restored in our churches.

Second, *God wants His church to restore its emphasis on disciple-making.* Jesus concludes His parable of the lost sheep with these words, "I tell you that in the same way there is more rejoicing in heaven over one sinner who repents than over ninety-nine righteous persons who do not need to repent" (Luke 15:7). His message is clear. The citizens of heaven are excited about anyone who comes to repentance. In 2 Peter 3:9 we read, "The Lord is not slow in keeping His promise, as some understand slowness. He is patient with you, not wanting anyone to perish, but everyone to come to repentance." God wants His church to make disciples; He wants His lost children to be found.

Any church that takes seriously its disciple-making mandate must be creative in its strategizing. We cannot expect typical nonbelievers to come into the church. We can't wait for them to come to us; we must go to them. We must design programs that will meet needs of unchurched people. Worship services, Sunday School classes, small groups, concerts, special breakfasts, luncheons, athletic clinics, and many other possibilities must be planned with the unchurched person in mind.

Every worship service must be appropriate in content and style so that people feel free to invite friends any Sunday of the year. At Sunset, we seek to make every worship service appealing to visitors. In addition, several times a year we plan special "friendship" Sundays. Our people have learned that these are particularly good Sundays to invite a friend. A large percentage of our people bring guests with them on these invite-a-guest Sundays. Making the church attractive for visitors will increase the likelihood of members inviting guests.

Studies have shown that of all the reasons unchurched people do not go to church, one of the most common reasons given is that they have not been asked. A church historian found that the average person in one denomination invites others to church once every twenty-eight years.[6] Surely we can do better than that. My wife Jorie and I try to bring a family or an individual to church with us most Sundays. We have many friends and acquaintances that have no church connection whatsoever. When we have an appropriate opportunity, we invite them to join us in worship.

When our youngest son was baptized, we made it an occasion to invite many friends to church with us and into our home. Friends who probably would have considered an invitation to church strange and threatening were happy to join us in worship for this celebration. I encourage our church members to use special occasions such as weddings, anniversaries, baptisms, baby dedications, acceptance to church membership, elder and deacon ordination and installations, graduations, etc., as opportunities to invite their friends to worship with them.

A church that desires to make disciples must also see to it that its members are not given too many responsibilities, or they will have little time left to cultivate relationships with their unchurched friends. One of the things our church tries to do to keep disciple-making a priority is to adhere to a one-person/one-job philosophy. We try to make sure that one person is not doing several jobs within the church. Taking on several ministry jobs is likely to cause burnout, rob other members from opportunity for involvement, and may preclude good ministry opportunities in one's neighborhood or workplace.

If you hold several positions or committee assignments in your church, consider gradually excusing yourself from some of those assignments. You may have more time to cultivate relationships with some of your work associates and reach out to your neighbors or family members. We give no awards at our church to the person who is at the church most frequently. We applaud the commitment, but we also recognize that our primary purpose is to send people out to make disciples. Christians have to constantly remind themselves that Christ's church is called to "reach out."

Third, *God wants His church to develop disciple-makers.* In Scripture, Jesus says, "The harvest is plentiful but the workers are few. Ask the Lord of the harvest, therefore, to send out workers into His harvest field" (Matt. 9:37, 38). There are people waiting to hear the Gospel. The problem is a lack of laborers willing to go out into the harvest. The wise church will not focus all its efforts on making disciples, but will set aside a large portion of its time and energies for building disciple-makers. It will give itself to building mature disciples who are equipped to go out into the world as laborers.

For example, it would be unwise for me, as a pastor, to spend all my time holding evangelistic meetings, passing out leaflets on street corners, going door-to-door sharing the Gospel, and speaking to my friends about Christ. Rather than trying to win the whole world to Christ by myself, my time is better spent discipling a few to join me in "the harvest." The fastest way to win people to Christ is by expanding the workforce of laborers.

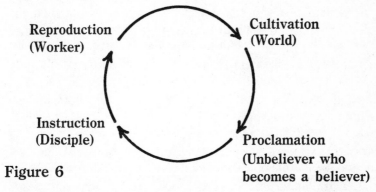

Reproduction (Worker)

Cultivation (World)

Instruction (Disciple)

Proclamation (Unbeliever who becomes a believer)

Figure 6

In figure 6 above we see that there are four parts to the cyclical process of making disciples: *cultivation* of relationships with people in the world, *proclamation* of the Gospel to unbelievers who become believers, *instruction* in Christian living to growing disciples, and *reproduction* of the entire process when disciples mature and become workers. The fastest way to increase the amount of cultivation and proclamation among non-Christians is to increase the number of workers in the world. Wise church leaders spend a large portion of their time building disciples who become coworkers in making disciples.

When I graduated from seminary, I accepted my first pastoral call to a church in Portland, Oregon, where my primary duty was to pastor the youth. The church began three years prior to my coming and had never before had a youth pastor.

There were only about thirty youth attending the church. There was no college or singles' group. Most of the youth who did attend were junior highers. In those first few months it was not uncommon for us to have only seven or eight high schoolers at our Sunday School and one or two for our Wednesday night Bible study.

Where was I to begin? One of the first steps I took was to find two high school guys who had a desire to follow Christ. Some time later I found two more high school guys who also loved the Lord and seemed eager to learn. I met with these young men two separate times each week. We studied the Bible, memorized Scripture, and prayed. As it turned out, I met with three out of these four high schoolers practically every week for the next six years. I was developing leaders to join me in the Lord's work of reaching others. Sure, I went to the high schools. I cultivated relationships with lots of high school young people. I shared Jesus Christ with all who would listen. But my most important work was with those four young men who were eager to grow in Christ. Those four young men invited hundreds of their friends on weekend trips, special outreach events, and to church during their high school and college years. They were the direct or indirect reason for scores of young men and women coming to Christ during those years.

During those six years of youth ministry, I recall sixteen young men with whom I met in small discipleship groups. The purpose of each group was always the same—to build those who would join in Christ's work as mature laborers. Of those sixteen students, seven went on to seminary and have become pastors. Most of the other nine are still following Christ and making an impact for Him. I can assure you that the seventeen of us are making a far greater impact for Christ in this world than I ever could have done on my own. It is worth the time it takes to nurture fellow workers. God wants His church to develop disciple-makers.

When Disciple-Making Becomes a Priority

A number of positive results occur when a church commits to disciple-making. First, *the church will experience unity*. When leaders communicate that the church body is giving itself to the disciple-making mission, and members join in this purpose, the church will enjoy unusual unity. Church members committed to a purpose no longer have time for backbiting, infighting, or gossip. They have more important things to do. They have a world to reach.

I believe our church has enjoyed an unusual sense of unity these last seven years because we have obeyed Christ's call to "go and make disciples." We have never strayed from this course. We know what we are about.

One of my associate ministers, who joined our staff several years ago, came from a background of church consulting. He had worked with all kinds of churches, most of which had problems to solve. He commented to me one evening, "One of the things I really marvel at about Sunset is the unity we enjoy. I have never worked with a church leadership board and staff where people got along so well together." I couldn't have received a finer compliment. We have enjoyed God's blessing and the same peace which Luke used to describe the early church—"All the believers were one in heart and mind" (Acts 4:32).

Second *the church will experience growth and vitality*. If a church body seeks to make disciples, people will be won to Christ's church. The constant and growing supply of new young converts energizes God's church and stimulates its growth.

The past eight years we have accepted over 900 people into membership at Sunset Presbyterian Church. We estimate that at least two thirds of these new members have joined our church by confession or reaffirmation of faith. In other words, most of our new members are not transferring from other churches, but are coming from unchurched backgrounds. They are new believers in Christ or are returning to their faith in Christ. These people are excited about their newfound or rediscovered faith. They bring energy and vitality into our church. The new believers challenge and invigorate the faith of the older and more mature members.

Third, *church members will increase in spiritual maturity.* In Colossians, the Apostle Paul writes, "And we pray this in order that you may live a life worthy of the Lord and may please Him in every way: bearing fruit in every good work, growing in the knowledge of God, being strengthened with all power" (1:10). Notice that when we bear fruit, we increase in the knowledge of God and are strengthened with His power. When Christians give themselves to disciple-making and service, they grow toward Christian maturity. This conviction motivated me to write this book. We cannot grow to Christian maturity unless we obey Christ's call to make disciples. We grow as we serve. We mature as we minister.

I'm not advocating that a church neglect meeting the needs of its members. Members need and have a right to expect good pastoral care. But one of the best ways to meet their needs is by getting them involved in service and in the process of making disciples. That is one of the surest ways to spur them on to the growth, challenge, and friendships they are looking for.

Try it yourself. Sign up to teach Sunday School. Become a small group leader. Invite a friend to church. Share with a neighbor what Jesus Christ has done for you. See if in the process you don't feel greater church unity, experience growth in your church, sense a new vitality in your faith, and increase in your Christian maturity.

Making disciples is not a high priority in many churches. Why don't you change that trend? Help your church keep its focus on making disciples. Help your church touch people with the Good News of Christ. Seek to make disciples and you will enable your church to grow.

NOTES

1. C. Peter Wagner, *Leading Your Church to Growth* (Ventura, Calif.: Regal Books, 1984), 44.

2. *The Summary Report of the Committee on Membership Trends* (New York: United Presbyterian Church U.S.A., 1976), 20.

3. *Omnibus* (Portland: Presbytery of the Cascades, Presbyterian Church U.S.A., August/September 1987).

4. *Statistics* (New York: United Presbyterian Church U.S.A., 1965); *Statistics* (New York: United Presbyterian Church U.S.A., 1985).

5. *Theodore Otto Wedel: An Anthology,* ed. William F. Lea (Cincinnati, Ohio: Forward Movement, 1972), 129–30.

6. Luis Palau, "Here's the Church . . . Here's the People," *Focus on the Family,* November 1986, 5.

PART TWO

The Strategy:
Elements in the Process
of Making Disciples

CHAPTER FOUR
Praying in Preparation

His heart was overwhelmed with sorrow. He faced the darkest days of His life. He asked three close friends a simple request: to support Him in His most difficult hour by staying awake and praying. He went a little farther and fell on His knees and cried out to God, "Father, . . . everything is possible for You. Take this cup from Me. Yet not what I will, but what You will" (Mark 14:36). Then He returned to His three friends; He found them all sleeping. He asked them, "Could you not keep watch for one hour? Watch and pray" (Mark 14:37-38). Jesus was greatly disappointed with His disciples.

If Jesus were to come today and ask one question of the church, I believe it would be this: "Could you not keep watch and pray for one hour?" The greatest weakness in the American church today is our lack of prayer.

We live in a busy society. Go to the airport, walk downtown, drop by a shopping mall, drive onto any freeway in America, and you will find that rushing is routine for nearly everyone. People are in a hurry. Businesspeople have meetings upon meetings. Pastors have appointment after appointment. The problem is that we've equated busyness with success. We're constantly trying to impress others with how busy we are.

In the process of living up to our "success," we have lost the art of serenity and the commitment to meditation and prayer. We no longer place a high value on solitude. This is one of the greatest problems in our culture today.

Our church leaders even fall prey to this great temptation. When ten to fifteen of my fellow Presbyterian pastors got together at Sunset for a time of fellowship and prayer, I asked each of them to share something about their prayer practices. I was amazed and disappointed to find how little time some of them gave to prayer.

Dr. Ron Jensen, president of the International School of Theology, interviewed 350 successful pastors across America. Nearly two thirds said they spend less than fifteen minutes a day in Bible study and prayer. Most of a pastor's time today is active, visible, and social, lived out in the public sphere. Little time is spent alone with God.

The lives of influential saints throughout history, however, are marked by a certain restful spirit. At the same time, they were remarkably effective. They seldom hurried. They took upon themselves relatively few projects. Yet in what they undertook, they managed to leave a mark in history. What was their secret? They learned the importance of many hours alone with God. They gave themselves to prayer. To be effective for God in today's busy world, we too must recover this commitment to prayer.

Jesus modeled prayer for us. He had divine knowledge of its importance. Mark 1:35 records that after a busy day, Jesus still took time to pray: "Very early in the morning, while it was still dark, Jesus got up, left the house and went off to a solitary place, where He prayed." Luke 6:12 tells us that Jesus spent whole nights in prayer. He prayed at all times, even after tiring days.

If Christ's church is not experiencing new conversions, there is most likely one overriding reason—prayer is lacking. If a church wants to see its neighbors believe in Jesus Christ, and if it hopes to multiply its numbers for God's Kingdom, it must be a praying church. Prayer is essential to the process of making disciples.

When Prayer Is Lacking

Without prayer, opportunities to make disciples are overlooked. Paul writes, "Devote yourselves to prayer, being watchful and thankful. And pray for us, too, that God may open a door for our message, so that we may proclaim the mystery of Christ" (Col. 4:2). He realized that prayer creates opportunities. Without prayer, opportunities to build relationships may be ignored or unnoticed. Chances to invite unchurched friends to church may be thwarted. Opportunities to lead men and women to Christ may be entirely subverted, if prayer is not a preface. If you have been frustrated in your disciple-making efforts, have you considered what may be the root problem—your prayer life?

Second, *without prayer, boldness in Christian witness is diminished.* The Apostle Paul writes, "Pray also for me, that whenever I open my mouth, words may be given me so that I will fearlessly make known the mystery of the Gospel, for which I am an ambassador in chains. Pray that I may declare it fearlessly, as I should" (Eph. 6:19-20). He knew he needed prayer support in order to speak for Christ without fear.

Acts 4:23-31 records an incident in which the early church was driven to prayer. Peter and John reported to the early believers that the Sadducees had forbidden them to share the message of Christ. So they prayed, "Lord, consider their threats and enable your servants to speak your word with great boldness. Stretch out Your hand to heal and perform miraculous signs and wonders through the name of Your holy servant Jesus" (vv. 24-30). After they prayed, we read, "The place where they were meeting was shaken. And they were all filled with the Holy Spirit and spoke the Word of God boldly" (v. 31). When we pray for boldness to share Christ, God always answers our prayer. When a church is not multiplying, we usually find that the people are not praying.

You might object, "Doesn't God want the message of Christ to go forth? Wouldn't He give boldness to any person who attempts to share about His Son? Why would He do so only if Christians have prayed?" The answer seems to be that God reserves most of His gifts for those who ask. Asking forces us to be dependent on Him and increases the likelihood that we will give Him the credit when the answer comes.

C.S. Lewis, in his Narnian tale *The Magician's Nephew,* illustrates that God works in answer to prayer. Polly and Digory, two children who have been ushered into the make-believe land of Narnia, meet Fledge, a Narnian horse. The three of them are discussing the meal provisions for them in Narnia.

> "I am hungry," said Digory.
>
> "Well, tuck in," said Fledge, taking a big mouthful of grass. Then he raised his head, still chewing and with bits of grass sticking out on each side of his mouth like whiskers, and said, "Come on, you two. Don't be shy. There's plenty for us all."
>
> "But we can't eat grass," said Digory.
>
> "H'm, h'm," said Fledge, speaking with his mouth full. "Well—h'm—don't know quite what you'll do then. Very good grass too."
>
> Polly and Digory stared at one another in dismay.
>
> "Well, I do think someone might have arranged about our meals," said Digory.
>
> "I'm sure Aslan would have, if you'd asked him," said Fledge.
>
> "Wouldn't he know without being asked?" said Polly.
>
> "I've no doubt he would," said the Horse (still with his mouth full). "But I've a sort of idea he likes to be asked."[1]

We pray, then God provides for our needs. The corporate church and the individual Christian who want to speak out for Christ must pray for boldness.

Third, *without prayer, commitments from new disciples will be few.* God has ordained that prayer be an integral part of the disciple-making process. The church that makes evangelism a priority will be a praying church. Without prayer there may be a good deal of activity, but lives do not get changed. Disciples are not born.

Most churches do not grow because they do not want growth enough to pray for it. Jesus said, "You did not choose me, but I chose you to go and bear fruit—fruit that will last. Then the Father will give you whatever you ask in My name" (John 15:16). When we give ourselves to making disciples, Christ's promise is to give us whatever we ask. He will give us converts, but we must ask.

Fourth, *without prayer, workers committed to making disciples will be sparse.* Jesus tells us in Matthew 9:37-38, "The harvest is plentiful but the workers are few. Ask the Lord of the harvest, therefore, to send out workers into His harvest field." The key to making disciples is to get more people out into the harvest. The way to get more people committed to disciple-making is to pray. When people are not inviting people to church or when there is a shortage of volunteer teachers and leaders, it is a sure signal of a prayer shortage.

Finally, *without prayer the spiritual power required to make disciples will be absent.* When Jesus was praying in the garden of Gethsemane prior to His crucifixion, He told His disciples, "Watch and pray so that you will not fall into temptation" (Mark 14:38). If we fail to pray we are more prone to fall to temptation. Absence of prayer spells a loss of spiritual power. Christians must never forget that we are involved in spiritual warfare. We are fighting against forces of evil. Prayer is the only means of disarming the spiritual forces that rule this world.

In Mark, Jesus describes Satan's binding ways, "No one can enter a strong man's house and carry off his possessions unless he first ties up the strong man. Then he can rob his house" (3:27). We have no hope of success unless Satan's stronghold over individuals can be disarmed. Unless this principle is understood, sincere and believing churches will never see disciples won to Christ. Satan fears nothing in our prayerless ministries. But his power is removed when we pray.

In years of ministry I have had opportunities to speak to many diverse groups. Often I feel I have the finest Scripture text to interpret, the most clever illustrations, or a polished presentation. Yet there are times when I feel like there is no significant response. Why? I did not prepare adequately in prayer. Too few were supporting me in prayer. There was no spiritual power.

On the other hand, I remember a speaking engagement I accepted to an all-city Young Life club. I prepared carefully but this time, in another way. I spent the entire day in prayer and fasting. I prayed for the high school kids who would be there. When I finished speaking, scores of teenagers responded. Lives were changed. What was the difference? The spiritual forces of evil were disarmed; I had spiritual power through prayer.

If we want to make disciples, we must become people of prayer. We must pray for people to come to Christ. If our churches are to grow, prayer must be the highest priority.

Becoming People of Prayer

There are a number of necessary supplications we must pray to build disciples. First, *pray for opportunities*. Pray for opportunities to show God's love to someone, to cultivate a relationship with an unchurched person, or share what Christ means to you with an unbeliever. God always answers this prayer. When I ask God to show me someone He wants to help or talk to, He invariably shows me many hurting people.

Paul instructs us, "Devote yourselves to prayer, being watchful and thankful" (Col. 4:2). Once we have prayed, we must watch for the opportunities God gives us. Disciples are made through the combination of prayer and action. It is never enough simply to pray; we must also be willing to be part of the answer.

Pray for opportunities to minister for Christ. Paul asked the Colossians to pray for him. Pray for your fellow Christians. Intercede for your pastoral staff. Pray for those who are in strategic positions of leadership to be witnesses for Christ. Above all, pray for opportunities.

Second, *pray for boldness in sharing with potential disciples.* Most of us are scared to death about telling someone else what Christ means to us. Many of us would choose to be quiet rather than take the chance of being offensive. That is why Paul tells us to pray for boldness. We need to pray to speak fearlessly—so our message will be clear.

Many times when I speak or preach, I find a number of things that might hinder the message from going out clearly: a poor sound system, distracting noise from another room, a raspy throat I might have, someone in the audience who is coughing, or a crying baby. When there are disruptions that distract people from God's message, I could become timid and conclude that people are bored and uninterested. But instead, I ask God to help me continue to speak boldly. I quietly pray for God to stop the distraction, so His message will be clearly heard and understood. Time and again I've seen Him clear my throat, solve a microphone problem, stop a cough, or pacify a baby. God wants His people to speak boldly of Him. He helps us share His message boldly when we ask in prayer.

Third, *pray by personal name for specific people to become disciples.* Pray for your family, neighborhood, and friends at work or school who do not know Christ. Pray that God will prepare their hearts to respond to the Gospel. Sometimes God will give you a strong desire to pray for someone. Pray fervently for that person, because God may be preparing a great work in that person's life. Pray for Satan's power to be broken in your school or neighborhood, so that people are ready to hear and understand the Gospel.

Several years ago, the house across the street from ours became vacant. My wife Jorie began to pray for the family that would move into that home. She prayed that they would be Christians or would come to Christ. Sometime after she began praying, three young, swinging singles began renting the house. Quite obviously, they were not the Christian family Jorie had requested. Jorie, who is part detective by nature, watched them carefully and figured out that they were doing a steady drug business. Several months went by before they were evicted from the house.

Nearly two years after Jorie began praying for our neighbors-to-be, a family moved in. Ron and Susan were the parents of three teenagers. When Susan and Jorie got acquainted, Jorie learned the following story. Their family had bought the home shortly after Jorie began praying. They had first rented the house to the three singles. Two or three years before they moved to our neighborhood, the family had been deeply involved with the occult. They became Christians a short time after Jorie began praying. During this period, the entire family came to Christ. One of their sons, Bryan, grew strong as a Christian and several years later began attending our church. He later became one of our youth interns and now is studying in seminary to become a pastor.

There were many forces working in the lives of this family to draw them to Christ. We don't assume they committed their lives to Christ solely because of Jorie's prayers. But certainly her prayers contributed to the conversion of that family.

Fourth, *pray for workers to go into the harvest.* The fastest way to see the Gospel spread is to pray for more Christians to give themselves to evangelism. Pray for people to grow in their faith and to get involved in some aspect of disciple-making.

When Jorie and I began in church youth ministry in 1975, we decided to recruit leaders to work with each of our youth classes. We divided the high school group into eight classes, separated by age and sex. I began working with the sopho-more guys and Jorie began with the freshman girls, the class of 1979.

The ministry started slowly but soon began to grow quite rapidly. All the groups met together on Sunday morning. The eight groups then met separately in homes on Wednesday nights. Each week I would take attendance. Three of the groups were quite large, averaging twenty-five kids each week. Four of the groups were medium in size, with between ten and twenty each week. But one of the groups was always small—the male class of 1979. Their attendance was always the same—two or three. When the class of 1978 graduated, I no longer had a group, so I decided to work with the guys in the class of 1979.

Where was I to begin? I used that summer to get to know the senior class. One of the men in the church let me use his ski boat, so I probably took thirty senior guys skiing with us during those three months. It really wasn't too difficult to get them to come along. Jorie and I always went together. She would take two or three of the senior girls with whom she was working. They were some of the most popular girls in all the school, so the guys eagerly joined in.

But socializing wasn't the first thing I did, nor the most important thing I did. I began with prayer. I made a list of every senior guy I met in the schools or at church, and I began to pray for them by name. Specifically, I was praying for stu-dent leaders who would join me in working with the senior guys.

By the time school started that fall, I had found three senior guys who had given their lives to Christ, showed a desire to grow, and demonstrated leadership ability. I met with them every week to study the Bible and pray. Those three worked with me all that year. Each week they made phone calls, passed out invitations, picked up classmates in their cars, and talked to friends about Christ. Because they gave themselves to the task of making disciples, they grew immeasurably in their faith. Together, we saw about a dozen senior men come to Christ that year. Between us we were able to get fifteen to twenty-five students to come out for the senior boy's Bible study every week that year. When it comes to making disciples, the most important thing we can pray for is fellow workers.

Fifth, *pray with faith*. Jesus said, "Have faith in God. . . . I tell you the truth, if anyone says to this mountain, 'Go, throw yourself into the sea,' and does not doubt in his heart but believes that what he says will happen, it will be done for him. Therefore I tell you, whatever you ask for in prayer, believe that you have received it, and it will be yours" (Mark 11:22-24).

Two principles help me pray with faith. I pray until I believe. The purpose of prayer is not to inform God; He already knows everything. It is to bring us to the point of faith. If I'm worried about something, I pray until I'm confident God will answer. Second, I visualize what it is I am praying for. I never experienced power in prayer until I learned to verbalize specific requests with God. I visualize exactly the answer I believe will bring Him the most glory.

During 1985 to 1987, our church was seeking two associate pastors. Each search took approximately eighteen months. During those long months, I got very discouraged. We read hundreds of resumes and interviewed dozens of people around the country, but nobody seemed right for us. I remember praying, "God, why is it taking so long? Surely there must be somebody that can come and minister among us." Then I visualized what we were looking for: someone who loves Christ, is God-fearing, believes in the Scriptures as God's infallible Word, demonstrates strong leadership ability, is willing to put down roots in long-term ministry with us, and (here's the rub) someone who would love me and enjoy working with me. I prayed until I was confident that God had such a person. Only then would worry vanish. Sometime later, God brought us two excellent servants. God answered our prayers of faith that He would provide the staff people we needed.

Finally, *pray with diligence.* You ask, "How can I pray more? I am so busy. I have no time." We are all busy. It is a matter of priorities. We all have time enough to breathe and sleep and eat. When we realize that prayer is as vital as these we will be amazed at how much time we find to pray. When we understand that disciples are not made without prayer, then we simply will have to pray. Prayer has been at the heart of every revival in the history of Christianity. We will never experience God's blessing without prayer.

We must give prime time to prayer. I pray while driving in the car, riding my bike, or swimming laps. Those are not the only times I pray. One day God convicted me that I was not giving Him premium time. I was giving Him the leftovers—praying while I was doing other things. Now I realize that fervent, heartfelt prayer cannot be shared with some activity. It requires my total concentration.

We must pray more with others. Jesus tells us that God grants increased spiritual power when we pray with other believers. In Matthew 18:19, He says, "I tell you that if two of you on earth agree about anything you ask for, it will be done for you by My Father in heaven." Pray with your spouse. Pray with your roommate. Pray with your children. Join a small group and lay your needs before God together in prayer.

Pray with other people in your church. Fifteen minutes before each of the Sunday worship services at our church we have a time of prayer for the services and various classes. I have told our people, "If people prayed before the worship services, if they gathered to pray for spiritual strongholds to be broken, we would see people convicted by God before I ever stand to preach."

Last year I received this letter from one of our members a man who was learning the importance of prayer:

Dear Ron,

Great sermon this Sunday. I was inspired when you talked about Luther and how he usually spent two hours a day in prayer—four when he was busy. It helped put it in perspective when you said he had six children. Being the father of one, I realize how much time is spent parenting. Six—wow!

Time in prayer hasn't been a real pillar in my walk with God lately. In fact, I've been coasting along, but not growing in my relationship with God. Thanks for hammering on prayer this weekend. God used you . . .

To make a long story short, your sermon helped to solidify the importance of spending time in prayer to grow in both fear of and love for God. Guess what, my desire to spend time with God has grown a lot since Sunday. Hard to believe it's only Tuesday. Seriously—Sunday and Monday nights I went to bed and I was excited to get up and spend a little longer time with God in the morning. God is answering prayers and giving me all kinds of energy during the course of the day. Exciting times.

I really need your prayers that this time in the morning would become the cornerstone of my fellowship with God.

Thanks,
Steve Irvine

How about you? Is prayer the cornerstone in your life? Don't let it be the missing ingredient in your disciple-making efforts. If you do not begin to pray, you will not grow in Christian maturity. I commit to making prayer more central in my life. Will you join me?

NOTES

1. C.S. Lewis, *The Magician's Nephew* (Harmondsworth, Middlesex, England: Penguin Books, 1955), 139.

CHAPTER FIVE

Living Obediently

A minister who was new in town asked a small boy for directions to the post office. The boy told him, "You turn right, go one block, then turn left and go another block, and there it is."

The minister thanked him and said, "You come to church next Sunday and I'll show you the way to heaven."

The boy shook his head and replied, "How can you show me the way to heaven when you can't even find the post office?"

There is undeniable logic in the boy's response. If a person cannot find a simple location, how will he be able to show others to a more difficult one?

This story exemplifies the reaction of many nonbelievers to Christians today. Many nonbelievers say to the Christian community, "How can you show us the way to the next world, when you can't seem to cope with this world? Show us that Christianity makes a significant difference in your life, then maybe we will believe it can make a difference in our lives as well."

We must remember that the unbelieving world is watching us. A changed life is one of the finest avenues you and I have of attracting others to Christ. They must authenticate our message. There is no greater advertisement for the power of the Gospel than a truly transformed life.

John Stott in *Focus on Christ* testifies to this truth. "The difference between those who profess to follow Jesus and those who do not should be startlingly evident. When it is, people are attracted to Christ. On one occasion a Hindu lecturer on educational subjects, addressing an audience of educationalists in South India, said, 'I see that a good many of you here are Christians. Now this is not a religious lecture, but I would like to pause long enough to say that, if you Christians would live like Jesus Christ, India would be at your feet tomorrow.' "[1]

If Christians lived in the way that Christ taught, people would flock to the doorstep of the church. A transformed life makes people thirsty for Christ.

Thus far I have sought to show that the church is called to reach out to make disciples. Christians grow toward spiritual maturity only when they give themselves to some aspect of the missionary mandate. We grow tremendously when we spend ourselves in service to Christ. When we refuse to reach out to others, failing to use our gifts in service to Christ, our spiritual growth is halted. Giving ourselves to disciple-making is essential to growing toward maturity.

Where are we to begin in reaching out? We must first become the right kind of people. We must obey Jesus Christ and allow Him to change our lives. As Christ makes a difference in our lives, we become walking commendations for the Gospel. A first principle in making disciples is this: *An effective disciple-maker must be an obedient Christian.*

Candidates for God's Blessing

Why must we be obedient Christians to be effective in making disciples? I'd like to suggest three reasons. First, *only obedient Christians are candidates for God's power and blessing.* From cover to cover, Scripture teaches us that obedience is a prerequisite for God's blessing. Any believer who wants to be used by God must be an obedient Christian.

Psalm 37:4-5 says "Delight yourself in the Lord and He will give you the desires of your heart. Commit your way to the Lord; trust in Him and He will do this." You and I may want to see friends and family won to Christ, and pray for God to bless our disciple-making attempts, but God promises to give us these desires of our heart, on this condition: we must focus our joy and commitment in the Lord.

The psalmist tells us, "If I had cherished sin in my heart, the Lord would not have listened" (Ps. 66:18). We may cry day and night for a neighbor or work associate to come to faith in Christ. We may plead with God to help us bring someone to church or for an opportunity to share our faith. But God does not hear our prayers. Why? Because we are living in sin. We do not obey God. We do not take His requests of us seriously, so He does not take our requests of Him seriously.

On the other hand, James 5:16 informs us, "The prayer of a righteous man is powerful and effective." God honors the requests of an obedient Christian. Obedient followers are candidates for His blessing.

Jesus instructs us with these words, "If you remain in Me and My words remain in you, ask whatever you wish, and it will be given you. This is to My Father's glory, that you bear much fruit, showing yourselves to be My disciples" (John 15:7-8). Jesus wants us to bear fruit. He wants us to have the privilege of making disciples. But His promise to bless our ministry is on the condition that we remain faithful.

There are many examples in the Bible of this principle. In Acts 11, we read that believers who had been scattered by the persecution in connection with Stephen traveled widely telling the message of Christ. Verse 21 tells us, "The Lord's hand was with them, and a great number of people believed and turned to the Lord." Many people became disciples because "the Lord's hand was with them." We will never see people won to the Saviour unless God's hand is with us. And God's hand of blessing will not be with us unless we obey Him.

In Acts 11:24, we are told of the result of Barnabas' ministry, "He was a good man, full of the Holy Spirit and faith, and a great number of people were brought to the Lord." Many came to Christ through his disciple-making efforts. The reason for his success: his actions were a reflection of his faith. The Holy Spirit fills all those who obey God and who have faith. The Spirit is able to bless the ministries of the obedient.

I do not mean to imply that people are won to Christ by our righteousness or good works—not at all. God is the one who draws people to Himself. No disciples are born apart from His power. But if we hope to be channels of His power and blessing, we must be obedient.

Disobedient Christians Turn Off Nonbelievers

There is a second reason for a call to obedience. *When Christians are disobedient to God, non-Christians are repelled from Christ.* When people who claim to be Christians live in a way that does not honor Christ, nonbelievers turn away from the Gospel.

Recently, my attention was grabbed by a news story on CNN about a church with 700 members that moved into the small town of Marshall, Texas. Marshall is a quiet town of about 25,000 people. The pastor of this upstart congregation began preaching to his people, most of whom came across the border from Louisiana, that the people of Marshall were living in sin and that the leadership of the town was corrupt. He stated his intentions to get involved in the politics of that southern town and take over the town, if need be, to correct its sinful ways.

Many people in Marshall were incensed that a newcomer would move into their town, pronounce judgment, and announce plans to take over. The people of Marshall were furious that a pastor who claimed to be a follower of Christ should lack kindness and grace. When we fail to love, we don't create an environment conducive for disciple-making.

David understood the principle that people are repelled from God when a believer's life is not congruent with his faith. After committing adultery with Bathsheba and murdering Uriah the Hittite, he wrote "Create in me a pure heart, O God, and renew a steadfast spirit within me. Do not cast me from Your presence or take Your Holy Spirit from me. Restore to me the joy of Your salvation and grant me a willing spirit, to sustain me. Then I will teach transgressors Your ways, and sinners will turn back to You" (Ps. 51:10-13). David knew that people would be converted when they saw that the king was serious about obeying God. He realized that his behavior deterred people from following God.

While we may not be as visible as David, we too hinder others when we do not live obediently. Part of the reason for our society's moral decline rests in the shallow state of believers' relationships to the Lord. "The fact is," warned Charles Finney during the nineteenth century, "Christians are more to blame for not being revived than sinners are for not being converts."[2]

Paul knew that disobedience among Christians becomes a stumbling block for the unchurched. Therefore, he gave this counsel to Titus: "Likewise, teach the older women to be reverent in the way they live, not to be slanderers or addicted to much wine, but to teach what is good. Then they can train the younger women to love their husbands and children, to be self-controlled and pure, to be busy at home, to be kind, and to be subject to their husbands, so that no one will malign the Word of God" (Titus 2:3-5). They were to lead exemplary lives so no one would have cause to malign the Gospel. He continues in verses 6-8, "Similarly, encourage the young men to be self-controlled. In everything set them an example by doing what is good. In your teaching show integrity, seriousness, and soundness of speech that cannot be condemned, so that those who oppose you may be ashamed because they have nothing bad to say about us." Again, the motive for an

obedient lifestyle is so that no one will have grounds for criti-
cizing the Gospel of Jesus Christ. We must be the right kind of
people if we hope to project the right kind of message.

Jesus says of Christians, "You are the salt of the earth. But
if the salt loses its saltiness, how can it be made salty again? It
is no longer good for anything, except to be thrown out and
trampled by men" (Matt. 5:13). Christians who are no different in character from other people are of little value in spreading the kingdom. In fact, they are a detriment to the spread of
the Gospel.

Gandhi graciously omits from his autobiography one painful
experience that occurred in South Africa. The Indian community especially admired a Christian named C.F. Andrews whom
they themselves nicknamed "Christ's Faithful Apostle." Having heard so much about Andrews, Gandhi sought to hear him.
But when C.F. Andrews was invited to speak in a church in
South Africa, Gandhi was barred from the meeting—his skin
color was not white.

Commenting on Gandhi's experiences in South Africa, E.
Stanley Jones concludes, "Racialism has many sins to bear, but
perhaps its worst sin was the obscuring of Christ in an hour
when one of the greatest souls born of a woman was making
his decision."[3]

Obedient Christians Attract Nonbelievers

Finally, *when Christians are obedient, nonbelievers are attracted
to Christ.* Put simply, the obedient Christian is a person who
makes it easy for others to believe in God. When nonbelievers
notice the difference Christ has made in the life of a transformed Christian, they want to experience the same trans-
forming power in their own lives.

Solomon understood the power of a changed life, when he
prayed, "May He turn our hearts to Him, to walk in all His
ways and to keep the commands, decrees and regulations He
gave our fathers. . . . so that all the peoples of the earth may

know that the Lord is God and that there is no other" (1 Kings 8:58-60). Solomon knew that if the people of Israel obeyed God, He would uphold their nation, and all the peoples of the earth would know that the God of Israel was the only God in all the earth.

One thousand years later, Peter picked up this same principle (1 Peter 2:11-12). "Dear friends, I urge you, as aliens and strangers in the world, to abstain from sinful desires, which war against your soul. Live such good lives among the pagans that, though they accuse you of doing wrong, they may see your good deeds and glorify God on the day He visits us." Christians are to live good lives so that even critical nonbelievers will be unable to deny the good deeds. It is because of our good deeds that others are drawn to give praise to God. Who we are and what we do, more so than what we say will convince the world that Christ is Lord.

Paul stresses that Christians are to live in a way that attracts people to the Lord Jesus: "But thanks be to God, who always leads us in triumphal procession in Christ and through us spreads everywhere the fragrance of the knowledge of Him. For we are to God the aroma of Christ among those who are being saved and those who are perishing" (2 Cor. 2:14-16). Who we are, what we do, and what we say ought to act as a fragrant aroma that draws men and women to the Saviour.

When I met Jorie, my wife, she had recently been widowed. She had married at age twenty-one, and two years later her husband died of cancer. At the time of his death, she was working as an art teacher in an elementary school. After only one week of time off, Jorie went back to her work as a school teacher. The other teachers on the staff were amazed at how well Jorie handled herself after such a traumatic experience. Teachers were impressed with Jorie's confidence after the loss of her husband. Jorie noticed that a number of the teachers on the staff, many of whom were Jewish, began to drift into her room after school to ask her questions and receive counsel.

She was invited into their homes and was able to share the difference that Christ made in her life. Her principal was so impressed with her that in his letter of recommendation for her he said, "She was above reproach in everything."

I have noticed that everywhere Jorie goes, people are so taken by her lifestyle that they become thirsty for Christ. That is what we are to be like. By our lives, we are to make people hungry for God.

Becoming the right kind of person is where we must begin in the process of making disciples. Obedient Christians have far more opportunities to point people to Jesus Christ, because they attract people to the Lord. They make people desirous of knowing Christ; they become like Christ in their dealings with others; they are redemptive in their relationships; they incarnate the Gospel by the way they live.

The Difference Christ Makes

Consider some of the ways our lives can be a good example for Christ. Working with honesty and integrity at work or school can be a tremendous testimony to Jesus Christ. It seems that so few people can be trusted to keep their word these days. In business dealings, we're always afraid of being cheated.

In 1984, the home we now live in was built for us. We took great care to specify every detail we wanted in the house. We felt that if we didn't put our desires in writing, we would get "ripped off." Sure enough, in some of those areas where we did not have the foresight to put a specification in writing, we felt we were taken advantage of. It seems that a handshake and, in many cases, a written agreement mean nothing nowadays. Few can be trusted to give an honest deal, to work with integrity.

On the other hand, several years ago, my father-in-law shared this story with my wife. He was the president of a plastics company in Chicago, Illinois. They were pioneers in the industry. His company used to supply all the plastic computer parts and tape recorder reels to IBM and 3M. Until his retirement, all IBM plastic parts were made by my father-in-law's company. He told Jorie that all his business dealings, large as they were, were made with a simple handshake. These companies had such trust in him that they knew a handshake would suffice. He did what he said he would do, when he said he would do it. That's integrity. It speaks well of Christ.

Consider how integrity figures in financial matters. Christians who have not paid their bills promptly, or who have not kept their word in business dealings, have left a distaste for the Gospel in many nonbelievers' minds. In an age of many bankruptcies, consider the surprise a creditor might feel upon receiving a check for an almost forgotten debt. Imagine the added impact the check would have if it was accompanied by a note asking for forgiveness and stating that God would not let the debtor rest until he had made restitution. That creditor would know the powerful difference the Gospel made in one person's life.

Your marriage can also serve as an example of the difference Christ makes. With the high divorce rate and the even higher number of unhappy marriages, a healthy, growing marriage is a marvelous testimony to the stability that Christ brings to relationships.

Christian teenagers living in obedience to Christ can attract people to the Gospel. A teen who is not afraid to stand apart from the crowd can be the deciding factor in convincing someone that Jesus Christ really is the Son of God.

If you have Christian teenagers in your home, encourage them to stand alone for Jesus Christ and make obedience to God the top priority in their lives. Their testimony is one of the finest magnets in drawing nonbelieving observers into a commitment to Jesus Christ.

Examine your own life. Ask yourself hard questions like these: Does the character of Jesus Christ show through my life? Does the way I live make other people thirsty for Christ? Do I attract people to Jesus or do I repel them from Him?

One of my favorite passages in all the Bible is found in 1 Samuel 12:3-4. Samuel has come to the end of his life. He is old and gray. He is standing before the people of Israel and invites them to review his life. He says, "Here I stand. Testify against me in the presence of the Lord and His anointed. Whose ox have I taken? Whose donkey have I taken? Whom have I cheated? Whom have I oppressed? From whose hand have I accepted a bribe to make me shut my eyes? If I have done any of these, I will make it right."

"You have not cheated or oppressed us, " they replied. "You have not taken anything from anyone's hand."

When I reach the end of my days, I hope it can be said of me, "You have not taken anything from anyone's hand." You were a person of integrity. How about you? Would those words describe you? Right now, why don't you commit yourself to obedient Christian living? Becoming the right kind of person is essential to the process of making disciples.

NOTES

1. John R.W. Stott, *Focus on Christ* (New York: William Collins Publishers, 1979), 143.

2. Walter C. Kaiser Jr., "When True Revival Reigns," *Moody Monthly*, April 1986, 21.

3. Philip Yancey, "Gandhi and Christianity," *Christianity Today*, 8 April 1983, 16.

CHAPTER SIX

Loving Others into the Kingdom

An interesting case was heard by the Massachusetts courts in the late 1920s. A man walking along a pier tripped over a rope and fell into the cold, deep waters of an ocean bay. He came up spluttering, screaming for help, then sank beneath the surface. He was unable to swim or stay afloat. His friends heard his faint cries in the distance, but they were too far away to rescue him. But within only a few yards, however, a young man was lounging in a deck chair, sunbathing. The sunbather, who was also an excellent swimmer, heard the drowning man's cries. The tragedy was that he did nothing. He simply watched indifferently as the man finally sank and drowned.

The family of the victim was so upset by this display of extreme indifference that they sued the sunbather. However, they lost the case. With a measure of reluctance, the court ruled that the man on the dock had no legal responsibility to save the drowning man's life.[1]

The implications of this case are that you and I have a legal right to mind our own business—to turn a deaf ear to anyone in need. While indifference may not be illegal, it is certainly not the way of love that Christ taught. Apathy, the refusal to risk involvement, is a prevalent sign of our times.

This story seems shocking, yet we live in a society immobilized by fear. Few are willing to help a person in distress, for fear of the time involvement, the danger to health and life, the risk to family, or legal complications.

Apathy may be the attitude of our day, but it is simply not acceptable for a Christian. It is an impossibility for the Christian given to the ministry of making disciples. In the parable of the Good Samaritan, Jesus told us that His followers are to help anyone who is in need. We are to love others in the same way that we would wish to be loved.

In Matthew, Jesus gave His disciples the command we know as the Great Commission, "Go and make disciples of all nations" (28:19). He also gave us the instruction we know as the Great Commandment, "A new commandment I give you: Love one another. As I have loved you, so you must love one another. All men will know that you are My disciples if you love one another" (John 13:34-35). We must obey both of these commands; the two go hand in hand. As we go out to make disciples, the message is Christ. As we seek to make disciples, the medium is love. The Great Commandment is the strategy for fulfilling the Great Commission. Without obedience to the Great Commandment, there will be no fulfillment of the Great Commission.

The challenge to love others frustrates some people who sigh, "With so many hurting people in the world, how can I possibly love everyone?" My counsel is to begin loving the people you see week after week. Ask yourself: Am I sensitive to the need of members of my family, people at my office or in my neighborhood? There is little point in focusing on loving strangers around the world if we are not acting in charity toward persons with whom we have daily contact.

When it comes to making disciples it is best to focus our loving attention on family and friends. A careful study of the New Testament reveals that most people in the early church came to faith in Christ through the influence of friends or family members. Andrew told his brother Peter. Philip found his friend Nathaniel. Cornelius gathered friends, relatives, and soldiers under his command. Should it be any surprise to find that most people today come to faith in Christ through the loving efforts of trusted friends and family members?

Over the past eight years since I have been pastor of Sunset Presbyterian more than 900 people have joined in membership at our church. I ask participants in each new members' class to share how they happened to come to our church. Eighty percent of all our new members tell us they came to Sunset through the invitation of a friend or family member. Scripture commands us to love our neighbor. Jesus defines "neighbor," in Luke 10, as anyone with whom we come in contact. In other words, we are instructed to love everyone God puts in our path. Since friends, work associates, and family members are the people God puts in our lives most frequently, and since most people come to Christ and His church through the influence of friends and family members, it seems wise to focus our disciple-making efforts on our close companions and relatives.

The Christian who wants to see people become disciples of Christ, must learn to love. The church that wants to see disciples won to Christ and experience growth must become a loving church. A wide-ranging study of members who had recently dropped out of their church found that the majority of persons said that they left their church because they did not feel needed, wanted, or loved.[2] *The church or Christian that wants to make disciples must love people.*

The Reason for Love

I want to consider four aspects of love: the reason for love, the standard of love, the expression of love, and the structure for love. The reason we are to love is *that the world may come to know Jesus Christ.* Love is the characteristic that will arrest the attention of the watching world. If we expect the world to know we are believers, we must exhibit love. You may judge the authenticity of a person's faith by the love he shows to all Christians. Failure to love does not mean I am not a Christian, but it means the world has the right to make the judgment that I am not a Christian.

John 17:21 records Jesus as praying, "That all of them may be one, Father, just as You are in Me and I am in You. May they also be in Us so that the world may believe that You have sent Me." He asks that Christians be united in love so that the world might believe God's messenger. In other words, our love will convince the world that Jesus is the Son of God. Our love authenticates our message.

Love causes a Christian or a church to become attractive. A loving church exudes such warmth and contagious love that newcomers are attracted. A loving church grows because visitors are attracted and members never want to leave.

One survey of several hundred persons who dropped out of United Methodist churches asked two questions: (1) "Why did you drop out?" and (2) "What would most influence your choice of a new church home?" Over 75 percent of the respondents said they left their church because: "I did not feel anyone cared if I was there or not." In response to the second question, the dropouts said, "the friendliness of the people" would most influence their choice of a new church home.[3]

If we want to attract people to the Gospel and see the church reach new people, we must put a renewed emphasis on love.

The Standard of Love

Jesus suggests at least two standards for our love. First we are to love, *as Jesus loved us*. In John 13:34, Jesus says, "As I have loved you, so you must love one another." Jesus is our example. He who came to us, took the form of a man, and gave His life for us is the standard for our love for others. Like Jesus, we must sacrifice our rights, serve others, and give up our lives for the sake of others.

When we begin to love people in the same way Jesus loves us, people will take a greater interest in the Gospel we have to share. When people sense we really care about them, then they will want to know what makes us different.

Jesus shares another standard for our love: "Love your neighbor as yourself" (Luke 10:27). We are to love *as we love ourselves*. In the same way we naturally take care of ourselves, we are to seek the welfare of others.

Many people have interpreted Jesus to mean that a person cannot love others unless he first loves himself. They cite examples of people who have low self-esteem, and use Jesus' words as a call for people to love themselves. They manage to derive from His words a call to love ourselves. This interpretation turns the intent of Jesus' instruction on its head. The plain meaning of Jesus' statement is that we are to love our neighbor.

Jesus meant that we are to love others in the same way we naturally look out for ourselves. Even the person with a terrible self-concept who criticizes and does destructive things to himself, does such things, I believe, out of a motivation of self-love. His destructive words or actions are made in the hope of gaining sympathy or attention from others. We all naturally care about ourselves. Jesus would say: Let that be the standard of your love for others.

When we love others as we love ourselves, giving other people the same consideration we are careful to give ourselves, we will find people attracted to us, and many opportunities to share the reason for the hope that is in us.

The Expressions of Love

What are ways to express love for others? The Good Samaritan instructs us here. Luke 10:30-35 records the parable:

A man was going down from Jerusalem to Jericho, when he fell into the hands of robbers. They stripped him of his clothes, beat him and went away, leaving him half dead. A priest happened to be going down the same road, and when he saw the man, he passed by on the other side. So too, a Levite, when he came to the place and saw him, passed by on the other side. But a Samaritan, as he traveled, came where the man was; and when he saw him, he took pity on him. He went to to him and bandaged his wounds, pouring on oil and wine. Then he put the man on his own donkey, took him to an inn and took care of him. The next day he took out two silver coins and gave them to the innkeeper. "Look after him," he said, "and when I return, I will reimburse you for any extra expense you may have."

Which of these three do you think was a neighbor to the man who fell into the hands of robbers?

The expert in the law replied, "The one who had mercy on him."

Jesus told him, "Go and do likewise."

We are told by our Lord that our love is to be like that of the Good Samaritan. I find in the Good Samaritan at least three expressions of love.

The first is *availability*. Only the Samaritan was available to love. He alone took the time to help the injured man at the side of the road. He took the time to observe that he was passing a man in great need. We will never meet people's needs unless we slow down to notice people who are hurting. When we pause to identify those who need our love we will find opportunities to show Christ's love. People are hungry for love. But if your schedule is anything like mine, much of the time we are too busy to even notice those who are hurting.

The Samaritan not only took the time to observe the injured man, he also took the time to serve the man's needs. There is little point in recognizing the hurts of our neighbors and friends, if we never take the time to offer a helping hand.

If we hope to have any success in the task of making disciples, we must be available to people. We must schedule our time more loosely so we will have time to show we care. If we spend our lives rushing from one activity to another, we will not have time to spend with others.

Even pausing long enough to speak to a neighbor or a stranger, can have a significant impact in another person's life, as shown by this story told by Ted Brooks:

Bad luck—the light turned red, and I was trapped standing at the corner. I prayed for it to change quickly. He was standing too close to me. And besides, it was cold and I was getting wet from the snow.

"Can I have something for my file, mister?" he asked.

This one was a crazy—no doubt about it. The grimy box under his arm gave him away immediately. Crazies always carry something, usually a shopping bag with handles. They can be unstable, but this guy looked pretty safe.

"Sorry, no money." I had repeated the old lie so often it came out automatically. I half expected to hear myself say, "This is a recording. Please shove off and don't try again."

"Have you got anything for my file?" he repeated. Finally, his message sank through. I fished in my pocket, pulled out a brochure, and handed it to him.

"No!" he shouted. Then, almost pathetically, he finished, "I don't have a file for that." I took it back and turned away. *Come on light—change.* I stepped over the curb to look for a break in traffic.

"I'm Howard," he said, "What's your name?"

"Mark." One syllable was all the information I intended to give. I had no desire to have some crazy calling me all the time. I knew people who had to change their telephone number to stop the calls. I liked my number. I chanced a quick look to see what he was doing. He had a pencil in one hand and was stooping to pick up a piece of paper from the snow. Just then the light changed, and I took off.

Halfway down the block, I slowed down and looked back. The crazy had just closed his box and begun to look around for a new victim.

A few days later, I was walking the same route when I noticed an ambulance parked outside a dingy alley. I joined the crowd of onlookers to see what had happened. Two attendants in white jackets wheeled their stretcher out of the alley. It was the crazy.

His face was showing, so I knew he wasn't dead. But as the attendants shut the door, I could tell by their conversation that he wouldn't stay uncovered for long.

A policeman questioned some of the people in the crowd but received no answers. Nobody seemed to care that much, not even the cop. It was just a little added excitement on an otherwise dull December day.

The cop raised his voice and asked, "Did anyone know this guy?"

Nobody answered. Finally, I volunteered. "His name is Howard."

The people around me backed away—as if my knowing the crazy's name made me a crazy too. The cop came over and began to pump me for more information.

"His name is Howard. That's all I know, sir."

"Well, at least there'll be a name for the headstone. Thanks for your help . . . Oh, by the way—would you take this for me?" He reached down and picked up the crazy's box. "I'd like to skip the paperwork on this one." He shoved the box into my hands and walked away before I could say anything.

Why would I want this guy's garbage? I thought. I looked around for a trash can, but . . . I couldn't just toss the box. Maybe it was the stories I had heard of million-aires who lived like bums, or perhaps it was just my slightly misguided sense of loyalty to the human race. Whatever it was, I opened the box.

I was disappointed. There was nothing but old clothes and a file folder.

I pulled out the file and dumped the rest of the stuff. Then I noticed the crude printing on the folder: "FRIENDS." I opened it and looked inside. It held only one small scrap of paper. On it was written "Mark."[4]

We live in such fear and move with such hurry that only one person paused long enough to share even a name with Howard. Even small gestures that take little time can make a significant impression on another person. Christians who want to love people and want to make an impact for Christ must take time to be available to others.

Another expression of love is *risking involvement.* The Samaritan risked personal danger by helping the man on the side of the road. There's always a risk in coming to the aid of a stranger or helping a neighbor. If we want to show that we care, we will have to risk involvement.

Several years ago I clipped this story from the Oregonian, of a man who risks involvement in other people's lives:

Postman Carson Bailey has become known as "Doc" to his fellow workers and some of the residents on his route. On one of his recent mail runs a Vietnamese family motioned him into their house where he delivered a woman's baby. After it started breathing, he summoned an ambulance. Another time he helped a woman who was having a heart attack.

On another occasion an elderly crippled woman was lucky that Bailey became suspicious about her well-being. "Her apartment door was always unlocked about mail time so I could open it and put the mail on a table inside," he said. "But this day it was locked and I wondered why. I peeked in a window, and sure enough there she was stretched out on the kitchen floor." Bailey and a neighbor entered the apartment and revived the woman. Bailey's only medical experience had been as a parmedic in the Army.[5]

What kind of person would do these things for other people? I had to know. So I looked him up in the phone book. I didn't reach him, but I talked to his mother. "Is his motivation for doing kind deeds for other people out of a religious commitment?" I asked.

"Yes, he is a devout Presbyterian," she answered. "He also has preached in a number of churches," she added.

Here is a man who was making a difference for Christ because he was willing to risk involvement in people's lives.

Another way we express love for others is by *serving whomever we meet.* It didn't matter to the Samaritan that he may have had a busy day planned. It didn't matter that the man on the side of the road was a stranger. It did matter that another human being was in need. The Samaritan's heart was prepared to love and serve any person in need.

In this parable we are commanded to love our neighbors, not evangelize them. It suggests that when we think of our neighbors, our primary focus is loving, not winning; caring, not converting; serving, not saving. When a neighbor senses we genuinely care, then he or she may be interested in our message. When we make service to others our highest priority, we become highly appealing people and have more opportunities to share the Christ who motivates us to love.

The Structure for Love
How can a church be structured so that it becomes a loving church? Let me offer two concrete suggestions.

First, *provide places where everyone can be loved.* A loving church must provide an ample number of groups within their parish where people can feel cared for, find friendships, and discover opportunities to serve. The larger a church grows, the more attention it must give to creating fellowship or interest groups. In such a church, everyone need not know everyone else, but people must make sure they are part of some group within the church.

A church that wants to be known as a loving church, will put special emphasis on creating small fellowship groups. Researchers found that people are most likely to feel love in a small caring/sharing group. Respondents were asked, "To what degree do you experience love from others in the group?" Seventy-four percent of the people in task-oriented groups indicated they experience a very high to moderately high degree of love in their groups. Twenty-six percent said they experience little to no love in their groups. Seventy-four percent of the people in Sunday morning Bible study groups said they experience a very high to moderately high degree of love in their classes. Twenty-six percent felt little to no experience of love in their classes. However, 85 percent of the people in small caring/sharing groups said they experience a very high to moderately high degree of love in their groups. Only 15 percent of the people indicated that they experience little to no love in their groups.[6] This means that a church that cares about love will want to get as many of its people as possible in small caring/sharing groups. In small groups, members can be the givers and recipients of love. They can be available to one another, risk involvement with each other and serve one another.

I believe that a healthy church should seek to have 75 percent of its members in small caring groups and should do all it can to get all of its *new* members into small groups. If you want to experience love and create a loving church, get involved in a small group.

Second, *encourage people and groups in the church to culti-vate love and friendships*. All groups, whether they are task-oriented like a choir or a committee, or fellowship-oriented like a study, prayer, or social activities group, should take time to cultivate relationships. The Sunday School teacher who says, "We don't have time for coffee and fellowship, we have too much material to cover," is frustrating the most important purpose of the class. People are hungry for love. They need to develop relationships where they feel known, cared for, and needed. They need to be involved in groups where they are missed when they are absent.

The person who develops multiple friendships within the church is more likely to feel it is a loving body and is more likely to be actively involved. The person who cultivates few friendships within the church will be more inclined to feel the church is cold and unfriendly, and will be far more likely to drop out.

A loving church will not only encourage love and friendships within the church, but will also urge people to love all people they meet throughout the week. Those church members will make themselves available to, risk involvement with, and serve whomever they come in daily contact. That church will reach out with open arms to needy people of all kinds—the poor, the sick, the lonely, and the rejected.

On Liberty Island, at the entrance to New York Harbor, stands the majestic Statue of Liberty. Millions of immigrants passed the Statue of Liberty as they entered the United States. For them, the statue was a strong welcoming figure holding out the promise of freedom and new hope. The idea of the statue as a "Mother of Exiles" is powerfully expressed in a famous poem written in 1883 by American poet Emma Laza-rus, inscribed in a bronze plaque at the base of the statue:

Not like the brazen giant of Greek fame,
With conquering limbs astride from land to land;

Here at our sea-washed, sunset gates shall stand
A mighty woman with a torch, whose flame
Is the imprisoned lightning, and her name
Mother of Exiles. From her beacon-hand
Glows world-wide welcome; her mild eyes command
The air-bridged harbor that twin cities frame.
"Keep, ancient lands, your storied pomp!" cries she
With silent lips. "Give me your tired, your poor,
Your huddled masses yearning to breathe free,
The wretched refuse of your teeming shore.
Send these, the homeless, tempest-tost to me.
I lift my lamp beside the golden door!"[7]

Would that inscription be appropriate on a sign in front of
your church? How about your home? Or your heart?

Both the church, and the individual who wants to make
disciples must extend a hand to those in need. Love is essential to disciple-making.

NOTES

1. Charles Swindoll, "What the World Needs Is Authentic Love," *Focus
on the Family,* March 1984, 6.

2. Warren Hartman, *Membership Trends: A Study of Growth and Decline
in the United Methodist Church* (Nashville: Discipleship Resources, 1976).

3. Warren Hartman, *A Study of the Church School in the United Methodist
Church* (Nashville: Discipleship Resources, 1972).

4. Ted Brooks, "The Crazy on the Corner," *Focus on the Family,* December 1984, 4–5.

5. "Neither Rain, nor Sleet, nor Baby," *Oregonian,* 18 May 1981.

6. Win Arn, *Who Cares About Love?* (Pasadena: Church Growth Press,
1986), 171.

7. *World Book Encyclopedia,* s.v. "Statue of Liberty."

CHAPTER SEVEN
Cultivating Relationships

My father and mother both grew up on farms. One of my uncles made his living as a farmer. On several occasions, our family visited his farm in South Dakota. I learned from him the importance of preparing the soil before planting the seed. A farmer must carefully burn and plow his fields before sowing the seed. No farmer would expect a plentiful harvest, unless he had first cultivated the soil.

After plowing the fields and planting the seed, farmers must be diligent in fertilizing and watering. Only if they are careful to cultivate the soil, plant the seed, fertilize and water, and are fortunate to have favorable weather conditions can they expect to reap a plentiful harvest.

Christians who want to make disciples can learn a great deal from farmers. I find that most Christians have a "reaping" mentality. We want opportunities to share our faith with nonbelievers. We want to see people become Christians. We are eager for friends and neighbors to come to our church. Our prayer is for people to come to know Jesus Christ, but there can never be a large harvest unless we pay careful attention to the cultivation of relationships.

To equate evangelism with reaping is like equating farming with harvesting. When we begin the process of making disciples, we must view our situation as if we were facing an empty field. Much cultivating, planting, watering, and fertilizing must be done before we can hope to reap a harvest.

Jesus told a parable that taught us this truth: "Listen! A farmer went out to sow his seed. As he was scattering the seed, some fell along the path, and the birds came and ate it up. Some fell on rocky places, where it did not have much soil. It sprang up quickly, because the soil was shallow. But when the sun came up, the plants were scorched, and they withered because they had no root. Other seed fell among thorns, which grew up and choked the plants, so that they did not bear grain. Still other seed fell on good soil. It came up, grew and produced a crop, multiplying thirty, sixty, or even a hundred times" (Mark 4:3-9).

Why was there a meager harvest in three cases and a bountiful harvest in the fourth? In each case it was the same seed planted by the same sower. The preparation of the soil made the difference in the size of the harvest.

The soil in the parable represents people. As Christians who want to make disciples, we should emphasize preparing people for the Gospel through the building of relationships. *The Christian who wants to make disciples will place a priority on the cultivation of relationships.* How can a Christian improve his or her ability to cultivate relationships? Let me offer five suggestions.

Watch for Opportunities

Christians who want to make disciples must *watch for opportunities* to build relationships with people. Paul tells us, "Be wise in the way you act toward outsiders; make the most of every opportunity" (Col. 4:5). To do this we have to cultivate relationships with non-Christians. We must be aware when opportune times present themselves.

Begin by identifying all the people you come in regular contact with who probably do not know Jesus Christ. Some are mere acquaintances with whom you may talk about the weather. Most will be family members, special friends, and associates with whom you are close.

Pray regularly for all these people. Pray that God will make them receptive to the Gospel. Pray for opportunities to build your relationships with them or to share what Christ means to you. As Jorie and I have prayed specifically for acquaintances and friends in our neighborhood and school area, we have been amazed to notice what God has been doing in their lives. Though we may not have seen them for days or weeks, we sense that we have grown in friendship and they are more open to us because we have been praying for them.

Next, take some steps to strengthen your relationships with these people. Share in a mutually enjoyable activity with acquaintances so that you can become closer friends. Spend time with close friends so that you can increase your mutual trust. Cultivate your neighborhood. It is my observation that most people don't know 50 percent of their neighbors. Invite neighbors or families of your child's classmates over for a party. If you want to increase your attendance, hand deliver the invitations.

Look for opportunities to talk with neighbors or work associates. Become an expert in small talk. Small talk is the foundational material of which friendships are made. I used to laugh at Jorie and say, "I've never met anyone like you. You can talk to anybody about anything for any length of time." Then I realized that is one of the reasons she has been able to attract so many people to Christ. We must watch for opportunities to talk with people about the ordinary things of life. If we haven't talked to our neighbors about their yards, houses, cars, or careers, they certainly won't let us in on the deeper issues of their lives.

About three years ago I met one of our neighbors. He attended parties at our home several times and we visited in his home a couple times for neighborhood get-togethers. He and I both enjoy tennis and played together two to three dozen times. He helped me on several yard projects. He came with me to men's breakfasts and tennis tournaments at the church. In all our times together, most of our conversations centered around ordinary day-to-day matters. He knew I was a minister, but that was never a major topic of our conversations.

A few months ago his wife walked out on him. He was devastated. He called, asked to talk, and said he wanted to start attending our church. If we are available to people in their day-to-day affairs, then when a crisis comes, they may well turn to us and let us in at a deeper level.

In addition to watching for opportunities to build relationships with people in your neighborhood, school, or place of work, ask God to show you other areas where you can be a witness for Him. As a Christian matures, he or she becomes more involved in the church. Free time is quickly filled with activities: worship, Bible studies, Sunday School, church socials, and committee meetings. Gradually you lose contact with your non-Christian friends. Church outreach events sometimes fail because members have too few non-Christian friends to invite. When that occurs, it is a sure sign that God's people are not looking for opportunities to develop relationships with unbelievers.

There are opportunities to build relationships everywhere we go. Consider the gas station attendants, grocery clerks, store clerks, and waitresses we see every week. Why not take the time to be friendly, get to know them by name, and develop rapport with them?

My barber has had a lot of problems with his two sons. Every time I see him, I ask about his boys. He readily shares with me all the difficulties he is facing and feelings he is experiencing. Through the years we have developed a relationship of trust. As I pray for him, I am confident God will give me an opportunity someday to share the difference Christ makes in our home.

Swimming lessons have become an annual ritual for our

household. Jorie usually takes the boys to their lessons, but once in awhile I draw the assignment. I usually take a book along so that I will not lose a minute of valuable time. Not so with Jorie, she has a more relaxed attitude toward life. When she takes the boys to their lessons, invariably she gets involved in conversation with other parents. Frequently, during a series of lessons she will develop a new friendship with at least one other mother.

A couple years ago she met one mother during a swim lesson series. They became good friends. Jorie invited her to attend our church. She came, enjoyed the worship, and eventually joined our church.

Be a Friend

A Christian who wants to make disciples will learn to *be a friend.* Look around and you will find all kinds of people longing for friendship. When you find such a person, be a friend and you may build a social bond that can become the basis for a spiritual bond.

Men especially are in need of friends. A recent study found that 75 percent of women interviewed could, without hesitation, name at least one intimate friend. More than 66 percent of the men could not. Researchers estimate that only 10 percent of the adult males in the United States have anyone with whom they can intimately relate.[1] Christian men can have a tremendous impact by reaching out in friendship to the men around them.

This past year, our two oldest boys compiled lists of friends they wanted to invite to Vacation Bible School. As they shared their lists of names with me I suggested that Tad invite a boy I had noticed the night before at a Cub Scout meeting. I observed that he had a large birthmark covering most of one side of his face. It appeared that other kids were not talking to him. It was my guess that he would be longing for a friend. Tad called his home. His mother informed Tad that her son was not home at the time, but she thanked him for calling and said he was the only boy who had called her son in the last four months.

When Tad got off the phone and told us the story, both Jorie and I broke into tears. It made us weep to think that this child would be ignored because of a physical feature he could do nothing about. Here was a boy looking for a friend. And there are many more out there just like him.

Find a person in need of love and friendship and be a friend. Most of evangelism is love. People don't usually care how much we know about Christ until they know how much we care about them. Building a friendship puts one in a position to share Christ when needs arise. Cultivating a friendship increases the likelihood of your friend seeking spiritual help from you in time of need.

The Apostle John instructs us of the importance of love: "This is how God showed His love among us: He sent His one and only Son into the world that we might live through Him. This is love: not that we loved God, but that He loved us and sent His Son as an atoning sacrifice for our sins. Dear friends, since God so loved us, we also ought to love one another. No one has ever seen God; but if we love each other, God lives in us and His love is made complete in us" (John 4:9-12). No one has ever seen God, but when we love, we show God to people. We make Him known through us.

A Christian who is seeking to be a friend must be patient as well. Cultivating relationships takes time. A child's mind is like a patio door—easily opened. An adult mind, however, is often like a bank-vault door. It may take months or even years for a friendship to produce spiritual results. Relationships take time to develop. Whenever a person moves, the process of cultivating friendships must start all over again. Christians who stay put in one neighborhood for a significant period of time are far more likely to be effective in the process of making disciples. People frequently come to my office for counsel about a possible job change and move. I advise people to be very cautious about making moves, because it slows down the process of cultivating relationships and disrupts family life.

Be a Servant

Still another way to cultivate relationships is to *be a servant.* In 1 Corinthians Paul lists several principles to help us become more effective in building relationships. He writes, "Though I am free and belong to no man, I make myself a slave to everyone, to win as many as possible" (1 Cor. 9:19).

When we make service to others a priority, we become channels of love that attract people to Christ. A serious problem for Christians today is that we have allowed evangelism to slip into the sales department and out of the service department. But when there is no serving, there is no selling. To become servants, we must become more observant of people's needs, and look for ways to meet those needs.

Pope John Paul II presided over the canonization of a servant and fellow Pole who had inspired John Paul to become a priest: Maximilian Maria Kolbe, a Franciscan friar who died for his faith—and to save another man's life—at the most notorious of Nazi death camps. At the end of July 1941, a commandant at Auschwitz arbitrarily selected ten men to be starved to death in reprisal for the escape of one inmate. Maximilian Kolbe, forty-seven, a political prisoner, offered to take the place of Franciszek Gajowniczek, one of the ten, who had a wife and two children. Consigned to a basement cell, Kolbe survived about two weeks without food or water, consoling his fellow victims with prayers, until a prison guard finally killed him with an injection.

After the rite, John Paul stepped down from the altar platform to kiss and embrace Gajowniczek, then eighty-one, who had wept silently through the service. Gajowniczek recalls: "I was never able to thank him personally, but we looked into each other's eyes before he was led away."[2]

Kolbe's service of love has had a life-long impact for Christ in another man's life. When we love and serve people they find Christ. When we serve others, relationships are built, our love is felt, and our message is heard.

Be Flexible

Fourth, a Christian who wants to make disciples must *be flexible*. In 1 Corinthians 9:20-23 Paul writes, "To the Jews I became like a Jew, to win the Jews. To those under the law I became like one under the law (though I myself am not under the law), so as to win those under the law. To those not having the law I became like one not having the law (though I am not free from God's law but am under Christ's law), so as to win those not having the law. To the weak I became weak, to win the weak. I have become all things to all men so that by all possible means I might save some." Paul tells us he had an adjustable lifestyle so that he might win people to Christ. Paul respected the scruples and traditions of whomever he was with; he had the flexibility to set aside his own practices as he encountered people with different customs.

We too must be flexible if we hope to win people to Christ. We must be flexible in our schedule so that we are available to people. We can never hope to serve the needs of people if we keep rigid time schedules.

We must exhibit flexibility in our lifestyle, as well, if we hope to reach people. When I'm with someone with a grade school education I tone down my vocabulary. When I'm with a vegetarian I don't eat meat. When I'm with someone who doesn't have a church background, I am careful not to use religious jargon. When I'm with a Jewish person, I don't order a ham sandwich. In my attempt to make disciples, I must show respect to the people I am hoping to reach. I don't insist that they change for me.

Without sinning against God, we must be free to go wherever necessary and do whatever necessary to reach people for

Christ. We must be more concerned about reaching people for Christ than with our own personal piety. Jesus wasn't known for His piety. He was known as a glutton, wine-bibber, sabbath-breaker, and one who hung out with whores. Without sinning, He did whatever was needed to draw people to himself. We follow Paul's and Christ's example when we broaden our interests and adjust our lifestyle so that we can relate to many kinds of people. To the best of my ability, I become an athlete to the athlete. To the musician I become a musician. To the artist I become a connoisseur of art. To the scholar I become a reader and thinker. I become concerned about whatever interests my neighbor. I do things I might not ordinarily do for the sake of cultivating a relationship. I become all things to all people, so I might save some.

Be Disciplined

Finally, in order to cultivate relationships, we must *be disciplined*. Paul writes, "Do you not know that in a race all the runners run, but only one gets the prize? Run in such a way as to get the prize. Everyone who competes in the games goes into strict training. They do it to get a crown that will not last; but we do it to get a crown that will last forever. Therefore I do not run like a man running aimlessly; I do not fight like a man beating the air. No, I beat my body and make it my slave so that after I have preached to others, I myself will not be disqualified for the prize" (1 Cor. 9:24-27).

Paul disciplined himself so that he might win people to Christ. Likewise, Christians who want to make disciples must exercise discipline if they hope to be successful in evangelism. We must eliminate those activities which do not aid us in winning people to Christ. Sacrifice unnecessary TV watching and other time-wasting pastimes. Guard against selfish pursuits that hinder spending time with people. Be selective in your choice of activities and disciplined in your use of time. Cultivating relationships with those outside of Christ takes lots of time. If we are to have the hours to develop friendships and serve potential disciples, we will not be able to serve on several church committees. We will have to limit our roles and tasks in the church so we have time to spend with neighbors and friends.

We must discipline ourselves, as well, to keep disciple-making a priority. It is easy to lose the urgency of sharing Christ with our neighbors and family members. We must remember that Christ has called us to Himself so that we might in turn share that Good News with others.

To make disciples, Christians must place a priority on the cultivation of relationships. Watch for opportunities. Be friends to people. Be a servant. Be flexible. Learn to be disciplined. Give special attention to building relationships with friends and family who may not know Christ.

Your focus will be more on becoming a friend than on winning a neighbor, more on serving than on saving, more on cultivating and less on reaping.

No farmer would think of sowing seed or going out to reap a harvest without first cultivating the soil. We must do the same if you and I want to reap a harvest of friends and neighbors coming to Christ.

NOTES

1. Win Arn, *Who Cares About Love* (Pasadena: Church Growth Press, 1986), 93.

2. Richard M. Ostling, "The Angel of Auschwitz," *Time*, 25 October 1982, 57.

CHAPTER EIGHT
Utilizing God's Spiritual Gifts

After World War II, German students volunteered to help rebuild a cathedral in England, one of the many casualties of the Luftwafta bombings. As work began, debate broke out on how to restore a statue of Jesus. Patching could restore all of the statue except the hands which had been destroyed by bomb fragments. Should they attempt to reshape the hands of Jesus? Finally a decision was reached by the workers. The statue was rebuilt without hands. But the inscription at its base was changed to read, "Christ has no hands but ours."

As long as I live, I will always be amazed that God is willing to entrust His ministry to frail and sinful humans. Second Corinthians 5:20 says, "We are therefore Christ's ambassadors." God has entrusted to us the message of salvation. We who are followers of Christ are the Lord's hands and feet. It is our responsibility to carry the message of His love to a needy world.

God has entrusted us with His Gospel message, and given us the necessary skills and abilities to succeed in sharing His love with the world. First Corinthians 12:7 reads, "Now to each one the manifestation of the Spirit is given for the common good." We commonly call these manifestations spiritual gifts.

A spiritual gift is a special attribute given by the Holy Spirit to every Christian believer for use in ministry. We receive spiritual gifts when we make a commitment to Jesus Christ. At the point of conversion, the Holy Spirit gives at least one, or, in most cases, several spiritual gifts to assist us in our ministry of making disciples and serving others within the body of Christ. Like talents, spiritual gifts are given by God, and must be recognized, developed, and exercised. While talents are given at birth, spiritual gifts are given at the point of spiritual rebirth. While talents benefit mankind on the natural level, spiritual gifts grow and nurture the body of Christ.

These spiritual gifts are described in 1 Corinthians 12, Romans 12, Ephesians 4, and 1 Peter 4. I do not believe these provide an exhaustive list. I am sure God has given Christians other gifts for ministry, but these are the ones listed in Scripture.

Spiritual gifts enable Christians in two ways: (1) they help us to love, serve, and instruct fellow believers; and (2) they help us to care for and reach out to non-believers. In one setting they build up the body of Christ (His church); in another, they expand the body. In Ephesians 4 Paul teaches us about this dual purpose of spiritual gifts. Verse 7 says, "But to each one of us grace has been given as Christ apportioned it. This is why it says: 'When He ascended on high, He led captives in His train and gave gifts to men.' " When Christ won His battle over sin and death on the cross, He gave us spiritual gifts to use in ministry. He continues in verse 11: "It was He who gave some to be apostles, some to be prophets, some to be evangelists, and some to be pastors and teachers, to prepare God's people for works of service, so that the body of Christ may be built up." Paul concludes his comments on spiritual gifts in verse 16: "From Him the whole body, joined and held together by every supporting ligament, grows and builds itself up in love, as each part does its work." Notice, spiritual gifts help the body grow quantitatively and build itself up qualitatively.

All too often spiritual gifts are recognized only for their value within the body of Christ. Most Christians have only been taught how spiritual gifts help them minister to one another. But the Holy Spirit has gifted us with spiritual gifts as a means of reaching those outside the body of Christ as well. Spiritual gifts enable Christians to minister individually and corporately to those men and women outside of Christ. The value of spiritual gifts in helping us to make disciples is seldom understood.

Spiritual gifts play a significant role in the process of making disciples. I would like to suggest at least three ways spiritual gifts contribute to the process of making disciples.

Spiritual Gifts and Ministry

Spiritual gifts help the body of Christ make disciples by making us aware that all Christians are called to minister. Paul instructs us, "Now to each one the manifestation of the Spirit is given for the common good" (1 Cor. 12:7). If each Christian is gifted, and the gifts are to be used for the good of others, then it becomes clear that all of us are called to minister.

That is the way it was in the early church. All believers, filled with the Holy Spirit and gifted for ministry, were witnesses for Christ wherever they went. Gradually every-member-ministry was preempted by a relatively few professionals. The task of the average believer became that of simply supporting the professional minister financially. How far that pattern strays from the scriptural model laid down for us in Ephesians 4:11-12: "It was He who gave some to be apostles, some to be prophets, some to be evangelists, and some to be pastors and teachers, to prepare God's people for works of service, so that the body of Christ may be built up." God's design was not that the professional minister do all the ministry, but that the professionals train the rest of believers to join them in ministry.

Down through the centuries, the church has always had to

fight to keep the priesthood of believers operative. There has been a tendency for the clergy to hog all the ministry. That trend still reigns. Many churches foster the mentality that the pastor was hired to do the work. People reason that the pastor was hired to take care of the congregation. He is paid to visit in homes and hospitals and to counsel the needy. Such thinking gradually leads church members to become spectators rather than ministers, pew-sitters rather than disciple-makers.

The church that acts on the knowledge that every believer is gifted by the Holy Spirit for ministry will see a steady stream of new disciples coming to Christ. A church with 100 people ministering will impact more lives than one pastor working alone, no matter how diligent or skilled he or she may be. Five hundred members who have devoted themselves to ministry will reach far more people than four or five paid professionals, no matter how resourceful the clergy may be. The Holy Spirit gifts us in different ways for various tasks, but we all have a role to play in reaching the world for Christ.

In a delightful scene from *The Lion, the Witch and the Wardrobe*, Peter, Susan, and Lucy all receive gifts from Father Christmas to aid them in their battles in Narnia. C.S. Lewis illustrates how the Spirit gives us a variety of different gifts for service in His kingdom according to His will.

"Peter, Adam's Son," said Father Christmas.

"Here, Sir," said Peter.

"These are your presents," was the answer, "and they are tools not toys. The time to use them is perhaps near at hand. Bear them well." With these words he handed to Peter a shield and a sword. The shield was the colour of silver and across it there romped a red lion, as bright as a ripe strawberry at the moment when you pick it. The hilt of the sword was of gold and it had a sheath and a sword belt and everything it needed, and it was just the right size and weight for Peter to use. Peter was silent and solemn as he received these gifts for he felt they were a very serious kind of present.

"Susan, Eve's Daughter," said Father Christmas. "These are for you," and he handed her a bow and a quiver of arrows and a little ivory horn. "You must use the bow only in great need," he said, "for I do not mean you to fight in the battle. It does not easily miss. And when you put this horn to your lips and blow it, then wherever you are, I think help of some kind will come to you."

Last of all he said, "Lucy, Eve's Daughter," and Lucy came forward. He gave her a little bottle of what looked like glass (but people said afterwards that it was made of diamond) and a small dagger. "In this bottle," he said, "there is a cordial made of the juice of one of the fire-flowers that grow in the mountains of the sun. If you or any of your friends are hurt, a few drops of this will restore you. And the dagger is to defend yourself at great need. For you also are not to be in the battle."[1]

Each of the children had a different but significant role to play in the conquest of Narnia. Likewise, each Christian in the church of Jesus Christ has a role to play in the process of making disciples.

A common misconception of many Christians is that they are not qualified to make disciples. They have been led to believe that evangelistic outreach is reserved for those believers who have reached an advanced form of Christian life. The New Testament standard, however, was that all who came to Christ and became disciples were qualified to point others to the Saviour. In many cases, those who accepted Christ, immediately began to share the Good News of Christ's love with others.

Understanding that all Christians are gifted for ministry will help a church make disciples, particularly if church members can structure their use of spiritual gifts to help the church grow. Most of people's time in churches is given to management, while only a small percentage of time is given to ministry. Church leaders must be careful not to involve everyone in roles that simply use their time in management. Instead, a large proportion of people should be encouraged to become involved in ministries that help people grow in their faith, reach out to the community, and draw others to Christ's church. A church can multiply its service to the community's lonely, aging, sick, and institutionalized by involving lay people in pastoral work. When dedicated lay people become informal pastors to neighbors and associates, far more people will be won to Christ. The key to making disciples is to get more Christians involved in the process of making disciples. Spiritual gifts help Christians realize that we are all called to minister and that we are all equipped to make disciples.

Spiritual Gifts Make The Church Healthy

Spiritual gifts contribute to the growth of the church in another way. *Spiritual gifts help the body of Christ make disciples by improving the health of the church.* It would be a mistake to draw the conclusion that all church ministry should be outward oriented. Yes, our ultimate goal is to make disciples of those who are outside the church. But to do so, the church itself must be healthy. We are unlikely to make more disciples and draw more people into the church unless the ones we already have are growing in love for God and each other.

Spiritual gifts help Christians minister to one another within the body of Christ. They help us serve one another, care for each other, and heal our brothers' and sisters' wounds. Spiritual gifts are the glue of love that holds the church together. In 1 Corinthians Paul tells one of the most important reasons the Spirit has given the church spiritual gifts: "so that there should be no division in the body, but that its parts should have equal concern for each other. If one part suffers, every part suffers with it; if one part is honored, every part rejoices with it" (12:25-26). They improve the health of the church by making it a more loving church.

Further, spiritual gifts improve the health of the church by helping individual members feel better about themselves. When Christians recognize their giftedness, get involved serving the Lord, and sense their value to the church, their esteem rises. Anyone who has gone through the travail of unemployment knows that one of the most difficult feelings experienced is the sense of utter uselessness. Spiritual gifts enable all believers to see that they are valuable and useful to the Lord.

Spiritual gifts also improve health in the body of Christ by helping people grow toward maturity. Talking about what happens to the body of Christ when spiritual gifts are in operation, Paul says, "Until we all reach unity in the faith and in the knowledge of the Son of God and become mature, attaining to the whole measure of the fullness of Christ. Then we will no longer be infants, tossed back and forth by the waves, and blown here and there by every wind of teaching and by the cunning and craftiness of men in their deceitful scheming." (Eph. 4:13-14) We need the gifts of teaching and knowledge to help us grow in our faith. Gifts of prophecy, discernment of spirits, and wisdom help us avoid error. Gifts of mercy, service, healing, and exhortation minister to our physical, emotional, and spiritual hurts. The body grows mature because all the gifts necessary for the health of the church are operative.

One key to a healthy and effective church is to deploy people according to their spiritual gifts. Since September of 1981, all the people who have become members at Sunset Presbyterian Church have completed a survey in which they indicated their spiritual gifts. Careful records are kept of the spiritual gifts of all of our members, so appropriate people can be sought when a need presents itself. We find people far more likely to volunteer for ministries when they know they will be joined by others with similar interests and strengths, and given a list of people who are gifted for that ministry.

For some time, we have talked of increasing our volunteer secretarial force to help our overworked secretarial staff. Our minister of evangelism and church growth asked one of our members to recruit and oversee that volunteer work force. We furnished her with a list of people who had expressed an interest in providing clerical assistance and a list of all those with the appropriate spiritual gifts, such as service, helps, and administration. She accepted the position because she knew she could count on some help.

When people minister in the areas of their spiritual gifts, the church is healthier and becomes more attractive to outsiders. Ultimately, it is able to be more effective in its disciple-making mission.

Spiritual Gifts And Disciple-Making

Finally, *spiritual gifts provide all Christians with a role in making disciples.* All believers can contribute to the church's task according to the areas of their spiritual gifts. As we discussed in chapter 3, there are four basic steps to the process of making disciples: (1) cultivation of relationships, (2) proclamation of the message, (3) instruction in the Scriptures, and (4) reproduction of the entire process. Those who are interested in making disciples will want to get involved as much as possible in all four steps of the process.

The good news of spiritual gifts is that God has gifted us in different ways. He doesn't expect us to be equally skilled in every step of disciple-making. Making disciples is a corporate effort. We pool our resources, possessions, abilities, and gifts to contribute to the goal of people coming to Christ. The bottom line in evangelism is to unleash every believer to do what he is gifted to do. Christians function best where they fit. Some cultivate, others sow, and some reap.

Some Christians will find that their greatest contribution to the church's mandate is in cultivating relationships. In fact, all of us can cultivate relationships with people toward the end of seeing men and women come to Christ. Some, however, with gifts of mercy, service, helps, or hospitality may be especially good at drawing others to Christ. There will be few opportunities for proclamation of the Gospel and few disciples will be made if there is not cultivating of relationships. Spiritual gifts provide Christ's body with skills for developing these relationships.

Others may find their greatest contribution to the process of making disciples is in the step of proclamation. Those with the gifts of evangelism, mission, prophecy, music, healing, or miracles may be particularly effective in this area. Miracles and healings have convinced many people of the authority of Christ. In Acts 5:12-13, we read, "The apostles performed many miraculous signs and wonders among the people. They were highly regarded by the people." The miracles gave credibility to the apostles' message.

Derek Porter, a missionary from Nigeria who was in our home recently, told me a story of some Muslims in Nigeria who were planning to build a mosque in a place where a Christian missionary was buried. They began digging up the missionary's grave when flames of fire leaped out of that plot of land. The Muslims fled, only to find that the flames chased them. They fled across the border into another country and even found flames there. This miracle caused a number of Muslims to come to faith in Christ.

A word of prophecy can also be a means of confirming the power of the gospel. In Hebrews 2:3-4, we read, "How shall we escape if we ignore such a great salvation? This salvation, which was first announced by the Lord, was confirmed to us . . . by signs, wonders and various miracles, and gifts of the Holy Spirit distributed according to His will." Prophecies, or words of insight from the Lord can do wonders in convincing people of the truth of the Gospel.

Not long ago, I read of one woman whose daughter had

worked in a quarry. She was in charge of the work shifts. When she blew a whistle the workers would come up out of the mines. One day she was working in her office, and she heard a voice calling her by name telling her to blow the whistle so the workers would come out of the mines. There was still another hour before she was supposed to do this, but she repeatedly heard the voice telling her to blow the whistle. Finally, without checking with the other members of the office, because she feared they would stop her, she blew the whistle. The miners started coming out. No sooner had the last one left the mines than an earthquake caved in several of the mines. If the workers had still been in the mines, the death toll would have been staggering.

The miners gathered around this girl and asked why she had blown the whistle early. She had to admit that she was a Christian and that she had just obeyed the voice of God. Hundreds accepted the Lord that day. Then, at an official inquiry, she gave a powerful testimony and many more families accepted Christ.[2]

Notice that this gift of prophecy was a powerful tool in sharing the Gospel with people outside of Christ. Signs and wonders confirmed the Gospel message in the times of the apostles, and they continue to accompany the message today. It is the duty of the church today to show that the Gospel has power. Much of that power is expressed through spiritual gifts.

My wife Jorie grew up in River Forest, Illinois. She spent every summer at a house in a place called Bethany Beach, Michigan. Karen Richards was one of her best friends at Bethany Beach. From birth, they spent every summer together at this resort. They soon became best friends.

After graduating from high school, the girls went away together to study at Wheaton College. They both married seminarians. Shortly after Jorie and I were married, Karen married one of my classmates. Each summer the four of us would meet at Bethany Beach. We all enjoyed tennis, so we had a lot of fun playing doubles together. God blessed us both with children. We had a boy; that same year, they had a girl. Then we had another boy, and they had another girl. We produced a third boy; they came through with a third girl.

Then, in 1985, Karen was diagnosed as having cancer. Eighteen months later she died. She left behind a wonderful husband and three beautiful girls.

Karen and Graham had the same everyday dishes that Jorie and I have. So each day, as Jorie saw our dishes, she was prompted to pray for Graham and his three girls. She prayed for them, just like she prayed for our boys. During these times of prayer Lori Williams, one of the girls in our church who babysat for us, would come to her mind. At first, she didn't think anything of it, but as Lori continued to come to her mind during prayer she began to wonder if God was speaking to her. She asked God if He was trying to communicate with her. Finally, she came to me and said, "Ron, do you think it would be OK to ask if Lori and Graham would be interested in meeting?"

I said, "Sure, what's there to lose? And if God is prompting you, we dare not stand in the way."

So, in January of 1988, Jorie contacted them both—Graham, in Illinois, and Lori, in Portland. And to our surprise, both of them seemed interested in meeting, even though the circumstances were unusual and they lived 2,000 miles apart. Letters led to phone calls; phone calls led to visits; and on Saturday, May 14th, 1988, they were married in our church sanctuary. A meeting and a marriage—without a doubt—arranged by God. As we look back we recognize that babysitting our four boys prepared Lori to raise Graham's three girls.

During their fairy-tale romance Jorie had opportunities to share this story with many of her friends in the neighborhood. These were friends who, to our knowledge, had no church home, and probably did not know Christ. Many people expressed sincere excitement each week when they saw Jorie. They said things like: "What's going on with the romance?" "How did the wedding go?" "If there is ever a case for God, this is it!" Jorie simply obeyed God by using one of the spiritual gifts God gave her, and it was an avenue of ministry to people outside of Christ. I don't know if she exercised the gift of intercession, prophecy, or the dangerous gift of matchmaking! But Jorie followed God's prompting and made people thirsty for Christ.

Other Christians are gifted to help in the step of instruction, as their primary contribution to the process of making disciples. Gifts of teaching, knowledge, wisdom, pastoring, exhortation, discernment of spirits, tongues, interpretation of tongues, and administration are some of the gifts the Holy Spirit uses to build up God's people and instruct them in the way of Christ.

Still others make their greatest contribution in the step of reproduction. People with gifts of leadership, intercession, giving, and faith provide some of the vision, resources, and prayer support to get as many people as possible involved making disciples.

All Christians are gifted. All of us can contribute to the process of making disciples according to our spiritual gifts. Not all of us are evangelists. Not all of us can proclaim the message of Christ with eloquence. But we can all cultivate relationships. We can all love people. All of us can make people thirsty for Christ. Each one of us can pray. Each one of us can contribute in some way to the health of the church. Whether it be mowing a lawn, typing a letter, baking a pie, sewing a dress, teaching a class, or sharing with a friend what Christ has done for you, all of us can participate in the process of making disciples. Do to the best of your ability what God has gifted you to do, and I'll do the same as God has gifted me. Together, as we pray, we will see men, women, and entire families come to Christ.

Remember, just like the statue of Jesus in the English cathedral, Christ has no hands but ours.

NOTES

1. C.S. Lewis, *The Lion, the Witch and the Wardrobe* (New York: Collier Books, 1950), 104–105.

2. David Wang, "Testimonies from Around the World," *Christian Life*, October 1982, 48.

CHAPTER NINE
Developing Christian Teamwork

Europeans who settled North America found it vast and unexplored. "Self-reliant" was their watchword, and the pioneer, with his axe and rifle over his shoulder, became the national hero.

In those early days, to encourage settlement, the government gave quarter sections of land to anyone who would homestead. People rushed west from crowded cities to claim a piece of property with elbowroom. Their first job was to build a sod hut to live in. We know that most families built their home right in the middle of their quarter section. The reason was obvious. People who had never owned land before had a new sense of pride and ownership. They wanted to feel that everything they saw belonged to them.

That custom changed quickly. This chosen isolation did strange things to people. Occasionally, photographers of frontier life returned with photographs of weird men, wild-eyed women, and children with haunted-looking faces. The survivors soon learned to move their houses to one corner of their property in order to live close to three other families who also lived on the corners of their property. Four families living together, sharing life and death, joy and sorrow, abundance and want, had a good chance of making it.[1]

Like the pioneers, believers learn sooner or later that the

Christian life is not to be lived in isolation. We need the encouragement and support of others. When it comes to making disciples we must learn to work in tandem with other believers. Far more people are likely to be won to Christ when Christians work together.

For example, consider the hypothetical conversion of a man we will call Joe. Joe is a middle-aged, married man with three children. He has a secure job, makes a good living, owns a comfortable home and two cars. He used to go to Sunday School as a young boy, but he dropped out of church during his high school years. Since his father seldom went to church, Joe saw no reason to go himself. He has not attended church for over twenty years. Joe's life has gone reasonably well without religion, so he feels little inclination to return to church. His decision to drop out hurt his mother who is a faithful churchgoer. Since the day Joe stopped going to church she has prayed for his salvation.

Joe has a friend Bob who has strong religious convictions and is active in his church. Joe plays racquetball with him every week. Bob has told Joe how important his faith is to him and has invited Joe to activities at the church. Joe has gone a couple of times, but he usually finds a reason why he cannot join Bob.

This past year Joe began working for a new boss—a Christian. Although Joe has not said anything, he has been impressed with the integrity of his new supervisor and the improved morale brought to their department. Some time ago Joe happened to see a Billy Graham telecast. The message has continued to linger in his mind. Recently he has found himself listening to a preacher on the radio.

Religious influences are cropping up in all areas of Joe's life. Joe's grade-school-age son has been going to Sunday School with a friend. Although Joe and his wife have never gone along, he feels religious education is important for his children, so he has been happy to allow his child to attend.

Last week Bob and his wife invited Joe's family to come to church with them. For some unexplained reason, Joe accepted. After the sermon, the pastor invited people to pray and commit their lives to Christ. Joe asked Christ into his life for the first time. Now he plans to bring his family to church every week, have them become members and get involved in the church.

Who's responsible for bringing Joe to Christ? The Holy Spirit, you reply. Only the Spirit can draw anyone to Christ. You're right. Or you might say his praying mother drew him into the kingdom. No spiritual victories are won without prayer. That is also true. Or you might give credit to the pastor. After all, it was his sermon that prodded Joe to turn over his life to Christ. Or how about Bob? He's the one who spent time with Joe, shared his faith with him, and invited him to church. Joe was brought to Christ through a team effort. The Holy Spirit used Joe's Mom, his friend Bob, his boss, his child's friend, Billy Graham, the radio preacher, the pastor, and undoubtedly a host of others to point Joe to Jesus Christ.

Evangelism is a corporate effort. Christ never intended disciple-making to be a solo performance. Thus far, we have seen that we must commit ourselves to making disciples if we are to grow mature in Christ. We have considered the importance of prayer, obedience, love, cultivation of relationships, and spiritual gifts in our task of outreach. Now in this chapter we will consider the importance of teamwork in the process of making disciples. *Disciple-making is most effective when it is a team effort of the church, the family, the individual Christian, and the Holy Spirit.* Let's consider how the church, the Christian believer, and the Holy Spirit work together in the process of making disciples.

The Role of the Church
The church is at the center of effective disciple-making. I question if we can make disciples without the involvement of

the church. Since our goal is to make disciples, and a disciple is one who is growing with Christ and gives evidence of that growth through involvement in a local church, it becomes clear that the church must be part of the process. How can a church help its people make disciples?

The church contributes to the process of making disciples by training and equipping God's people for ministry. The church, which Scripture calls the body of Christ, prepares people for ministry. It helps Christians be more productive in their efforts at making disciples by helping them identify their spiritual gifts. The church enables believers to have a greater impact by teaching them the importance of teamwork.

The church further contributes to the process of making disciples by instilling in its members a vision and motivation for outreach. It not only shows them how to reach out but provides them with the necessary organization, support, and accountability to be successful. The church provides small caring groups where people can find the nurture and prayer support they need to reach out to others. Growing churches give their members support by constructing buildings that are large enough so people can feel free to invite their friends. Churches offer support by creating an atmosphere of love that welcomes guests. When church members exhibit genuine love, unchurched people are irresistibly attracted.

Churches interested in fulfilling Christ's commission support their people's evangelistic efforts by providing programs to which members can invite their friends. We have found at Sunset Presbyterian that the best way to make disciples is to invite friends to church before they have made a commitment to Christ. We are discovering that when a person has no meaningful contact with the church in the process of conversion, one is unlikely to feel any meaningful sense of identification with the church after conversion and therefore less apt to attend church. Our strategy should not be to lead people to Christ and then bring them to church. Rather, we should bring them to church as part of our attempt to point them to Christ. The church which understands this principle provides programs to attract unchurched people; in this way it assists members in their efforts at making disciples.

The Role of the Family

The family is central in God's plan of spreading the Gospel. From the beginning when God created Adam and Eve and started the first human home, the family has been the basic unit in society. Take away the family and you destroy the fabric of society. It is in the home that parents pass on to their children morals, values, and religion. A church that wants to reach people for Christ cannot afford to overlook the influence of the family in formulating its strategy for making disciples. There are at least three ways the church can involve the family in its attempts at making disciples.

First, *the church must recognize that in God's plan Christian parents have the primary responsibility of passing the faith on to their children.* In one of his final addresses to the Israelites before they entered the Promised Land, Moses gave these instructions to parents: *Love the Lord your God with all your heart and with all your soul and with all your strength. These commandments that I give you today are to be upon your hearts. Impress them on your children. Talk about them when you sit at home and when you walk along the road, when you lie down and when you get up* (Deut. 6:5-7).

Parents are to teach God's principles to their own children. Churches that understand the centrality of the family will be careful not to supplant parents in their attempts at making disciples. Rather, they will equip and encourage parents to provide their children with spiritual nurture. They will instruct parents in how to lead their children to Christ and into Christian maturity.

My wife and I have known the privilege of leading four of our five boys to Christ. (Our fifth son is still an infant. By

God's grace we pray his day of decision will soon come as well.) If all Christian parents are successful in making disciples of their children the church will take a giant step forward in passing the Gospel on to the next generation. One of the greatest failures in the church of past generations has been children rejecting the faith of their parents.

Second, *the church can encourage family members to work together toward the end of sharing Christ with other families.* My wife and I have found that we are more successful in reaching other families when we work together as a family. Together we pray for whole families to come to Christ and our church. There are a number of families whose children are friends with our boys while my wife and I enjoy friendships with the parents. As our children strengthen their bonds with other children and we get better acquainted with their parents we increase the likelihood of winning an entire family to Christ. We work together as a family at disciple-making. If our children bring other kids to our church's youth program or Sunday School and we as parents do not at the same time encourage their parents to come to church, we decrease the likelihood of the children becoming disciples. People are more likely to become disciples and grow as Christians when their whole family unit comes to Christ.

Recognizing the importance of the family, *churches that are serious about making disciples structure their programs to meet the needs of the family.* They are "family sensitive" as they plan activities. For example, our church seeks to provide quality classes for all ages—children, youth and adults—on Sunday morning. There are groups for collegians, singles, parents, and senior citizens, so we can attract the entire family. We try to put most of our midweek activities on one night so that we do not fragment the home. Choir rehearsals, junior high, high school and college groups, children's programs and adult Bible studies are all scheduled on Wednesday night so families can come to church together if they choose. Nursery care is available for all church functions so we don't inadvertently exclude young parents. Youth and children's leaders cultivate the support of the parents. They realize that none of their programs can succeed unless parents allow their children to come and provide transportation.

During our "friendship Sundays" we encourage our children's, youth and adult departments to also have an outreach emphasis. This way church members of all ages, the entire family, can work together on our common task of making disciples. We recognize the family is one of our most valuable allies in making disciples.

The Individual Christian's Role

There are a variety of ways Christians can show teamwork in the process of making disciples. Teamwork in disciple-making is a great encouragement to other Christians. Encouraging fellow Christians through teamwork is one of the most important things you can do to reach this world for Christ. You can encourage your brothers and sisters in Christ in their disciple-making efforts through a number of means.

First, *encourage each other to remember making disciples is an urgent matter.* In case you've been tempted to believe that sharing the news of Christ with others is not your responsibility, look at what God says to Ezekiel:

Son of man, I have made you a watchman for the house of Israel; so hear the word I speak and give them warning from me. When I say to a wicked man, "You will surely die," and you do not warn him or speak out to dissuade him from his evil ways in order to save his life, that wicked man will die for his sin, and I will hold you accountable for his blood. But if you do warn the wicked man and he does not turn from his wickedness or from his evil ways, he will die for his sin; but you will have saved yourself.

Again, when a righteous man turns from his righteousness and does evil, and I put a stumbling block before him, he will die. Since you did not warn him, he will die for his sin. The righteous things he did will not be remembered, and I will hold you accountable for his blood. But if you do warn the righteous man not to sin and he does not sin, he will surely live because he took warning, and you will have saved yourself (Ezek. 3:17-21).

Like Ezekiel of old, we hold the words of eternal life in our hands. If we do not share the Good News, God holds us responsible. Paul asks us "How, then, can they call on the One they have not believed in? And how can they believe in the One of whom they have not heard? And how can they hear without someone preaching to them?" (Rom. 10:14). We know the answer. People cannot know of Christ unless we tell them. We must remind our Christian brothers and sisters that we have an urgent need to share the news of Christ with others.

Second, *encourage each other to remember that Christian growth comes through making disciples.* The book of Acts tells us of the rapid growth of the early church. There are nineteen references in the Book of Acts to the numerical growth of the church. New Testament Christians were growth-oriented. As they gave their energies to making disciples, they experienced rapid spiritual growth. There seems to be a positive relationship between outreach and the development of an in-depth quality of spiritual-mindedness.

Building a large church is not a proper motivation for evangelism. We make disciples because Christ has commanded us to do so. As a pastor I am sometimes criticized for emphasizing evangelism more than nurture and spiritual growth. The criticism is valid if we stress evangelism at the expense of nurture. The church must keep nurture and outreach in balance. I reaffirm the importance of evangelism, however, because I believe it is the key that unlocks the door to spiritual growth and maturity. We grow as we minister. The New Testament formula is not to mature and then reach out; it is to reach out in order to mature.

After Jesus delivered a man from demon possession, He didn't tell him to go home and study his Bible and take Christian education classes. He said, "Go home to your family and tell them how much the Lord has done for you, and how He has had mercy on you" (Mark 5:19). Jesus told the new believer to do this for He knew that in the process the man would grow in faith. We must remind each other to make disciples if we hope to grow toward Christian maturity.

Third, *encourage each other to pursue an exemplary lifestyle.* I ask each membership class why more Christians do not share their faith with people. One answer I receive is that Christians feel unworthy to talk about their faith. They realize they may have compromised in their lifestyle and are probably as secular as other people in the world. They feel that if they speak out about being a Christian they could be charged with hypocrisy.

Nothing destroys Christian witness as quickly as guilt. So if we want to see the Gospel go forward we must encourage each other to obey Christ. The writer of Hebrews counsels us: "Encourage one another daily . . . so that none of you may be hardened by sin's deceitfulness" (3:13). We need to encourage each other to obey God and avoid sin, for no Christian living in sin is free to witness for Christ.

When we urge people to attend Sunday School classes or small groups, and to be regular in their worship attendance, we increase the likelihood of them pursuing obedient living.

John MacArthur tells the story of a pastor who visited an unfaithful church attender. The man was sitting before a fire watching the warm glow of the coals. It was a cold winter day, but the coals were red-hot, and the fire was warm. The pastor pleaded with the man to be more faithful in meeting with the people of God, but the man didn't seem to be getting the message.

The pastor took the tongs beside the fireplace, pulled open the screen, reached in, and began to separate the coals. When none of the coals were touching the others, in a matter of moments their fire went out. "That's what's happening in your life," he told the man. "As soon as you isolate yourself from God's people, the fire goes out." The man got the message.[2] Meeting regularly with God's people increases the likelihood that we will obey Christ. Obedience shows the world that Jesus changes lives and attracts people to Christ.

Fourth, *encourage each other to continue in the task of making disciples.* If you are like me, you are quick to become discouraged when things do not go well. Many activities compete for your time, so it's easy for you to misplace priorities. You need someone to encourage you to keep making disciples. This is one reason I believe the Lord sent His disciples two by two. When one got discouraged and ready to quit, the other would encourage him to keep going.

The wisdom writer understood this principle when he wrote: "Two are better than one, because they have a good return for their work: If one falls down, his friend can help him up. But pity the man who falls and has no one to help him up! . . . Though one may be overpowered, two can defend themselves. A cord of three strands is not quickly broken" (Ecc. 4:9-10, 12).

Each of the past fourteen years I have participated in at least one caring group with four to eight other men. One purpose of these groups has been to enable each member to do a better job of reaching out to friends and neighbors. I have experienced the power of my brothers' prayers as I spoke to a Kiwanis Club or high school class, or when we have neighbors over for dinner. We have all improved in our ability to make disciples by making ourselves accountable to one another. We're more likely to reach out to our friends when we know that each week members of the group are going to ask us how we progressed in our disciple-making. The probability of

Christians continuing as disciple-makers is greatly increased if they are part of a small group that holds them accountable. If you want to make a greater impact for Christ, make room in your schedule to join a small caring group.

A fifth way Christians can use teamwork in disciple-making is to *encourage each other to pool their spiritual gifts.* Scripture teaches that every believer receives at least one spiritual gift when he becomes a child of God. Paul tells us how he used his gifts in teamwork with other Christians: "I planted the seed, Apollos watered it, but God made it grow. The man who plants and the man who waters have one purpose, and each will be rewarded according to his own labor" (1 Cor. 3:6, 8). In the process of making disciples many gifts are needed. Some Christians cultivate, others sow the seed, some water and others reap. None of us can do it all and we are not expected to. That is welcome news. Reaching your neighbor or work associate for Christ doesn't depend on you alone. The whole body of Christ works together to draw men and women to Christ.

Suppose a woman in your neighborhood loses her husband to cancer. Your church can reach out effectively to this bereaved widow through pooling a number of spiritual gifts. A Christian with the gift of mercy can comfort her. Another with the gift of service can help clean her house or take care of her yard. A believer with the gift of giving could give her financial counsel or assistance. Many Christians working together will give her a far fuller picture of the richness in God's love.

A sixth way we use teamwork in disciple-making is to *encourage each other to build on another's efforts.* Paul writes, "By the grace God has given me, I laid a foundation as an expert builder, and someone else is building on it" (1 Cor. 3:10). Don't ever feel you are working alone. You are building upon someone else's efforts. Jesus said, "Thus the saying 'One sows and another reaps' is true. I sent you to reap what you have not worked for. Others have done the hard work, and you have reaped the benefits of their labor" (John 4:37-38). When someone comes to Christ it is almost always through a team effort.

When Jorie was pregnant with Luke, our third child, she had to be in bed most of the pregnancy. Many people from the church helped us with childcare, house cleaning, and meals. Our next-door neighbor was amazed that people would give up their time to help us the way they did. She couldn't believe that so many kind and considerate people would serve us in our time of need. Each person who came to our home assisted us in our efforts at reaching out to our next-door neighbor. They all played a part on the team that pointed our friend to Christ.

Evangelism is a corporate effort. Kindred spirits pool their resources, spiritual gifts, time, and abilities to win friends and mutual acquaintances to Christ. Whenever you bring a friend to church, introduce your guest to others. When people introduce their guests to you, show the same interest and consideration as you would want them to show people you bring to church. In this way, we can share in each other's disciple-making efforts.

The Role Of The Holy Spirit

Christians cannot hope to see any disciples born apart from reliance upon the Holy Spirit. The Holy Spirit is the driving force behind all evangelism. The book of Acts could just as well be called "The Acts of the Holy Spirit in Building Christ's Church." It was the Holy Spirit who motivated the early Christians to share the Gospel message and who empowered them to reach out with Christ's love.

To say that no one can come to Christ without the work of the Holy Spirit in no way denies human responsibility. God has entrusted His message into the hands of men and women. Few people can testify that they came to Christ through the work of the Holy Spirit alone—without any human influence.

Yet at the same time, we must recognize that making disciples is spiritual work, and we can never do God's work without God's power. Any attempt at evangelism that does not find its source of power in the Holy Spirit will ultimately be misguided or futile. There are several functions the Holy Spirit fills in the process of making disciples.

First, *the Holy Spirit convicts men and women of sin and convinces them that Jesus Christ is the Son of God.* Jesus taught, "He [the Holy Spirit] will convict the world of guilt in regard to sin and righteousness and judgment: in regard to sin, because men do not believe in Me" (John 16:8-9). Paul taught that, "No one can say, 'Jesus is Lord,' except by the Holy Spirit" (1 Cor. 12:3).

Billy Graham tells a story that illustrates the essential role of the Holy Spirit. "During one of our London Crusades, a Russian nobleman came one evening. He spoke no English. Yet when the invitation was given to receive Christ he responded. The trained, Russian-speaking counselor asked him how, knowing no English, he had understood enough of the message to respond so intelligently. 'When I entered this place,' the nobleman replied, 'I was overwhelmed with a longing for God. Tell me, how can I find Him?' "[3] The Spirit draws people to the Saviour.

The Holy Spirit also convicts Christians of their need to pray. Scripture teaches that there are spiritual forces of evil in this world. These powers blind unbelievers from the truth of Christ. The Bible tells us these Satanic hosts maintain strongholds of sin that keep people from Jesus Christ. In Ephesians 6:11-12 we read, "Put on the full armor of God so that you can take your stand against the devil's schemes. For our struggle is not against flesh and blood, but against the rulers, against the authorities, against the powers of this dark world and against the spiritual forces of evil in the heavenly realms." Our struggle is against unseen spiritual enemies. In 2 Corinthians 10:3-4 we read, "For though we live in the world, we do not wage war as the world does. The weapons we fight with are not the weapons of the world. On the contrary, they have divine power to tear down strongholds." As Christians begin to pray, spiritual strongholds are broken and men and women are won to Christ.

The Holy Spirit also empowers Christians to share their faith. In Acts 1:8 we are told, "You will receive power when the Holy Spirit comes on you; and you will be My witnesses." In Acts 2 we find that the first sign of Christians filled with the Holy Spirit was that they proclaimed the Word of God. Filled with the Holy Spirit, they proclaimed the Gospel in tongues understandable to their listeners. In Acts 4:31 we read, "And they were all filled with the Holy Spirit and spoke the Word of God boldly." The Holy Spirit wants to see people come to know Jesus Christ. When we are filled with the Holy Spirit we are motivated to share the news about Christ. Disciple-making is a team effort; there can be no team victory without the team captain—the Holy Spirit.

Teamwork

Disciple-making is most effective when it is a team effort by the church, the family, the individual believer, and the Holy Spirit. Making disciples does not depend on you alone, but you are an important member of the team. Every Christian has something to contribute in our attempts to spread the news of Christ's love.

Peter Marshall spoke once of the importance of teamwork in winning battles: "The Battle of Britain which lasted from August 8th to October 31st, 1940 cost the Germans 2,375 planes destroyed in daylight alone, and many more at night. It cost the British 375 pilots killed and 358 wounded. A handful of RAF fliers had saved Britain, and perhaps the world, from destruction.

"Do you remember how Winston Churchill spoke for his people: 'Never in the field of human conflict was so much owed by so many to so few!' That victory was achieved you see, not by the top-ranking generals, the brass hats, the big shots, but by young men—a team—playing and fighting . . . and dying together."[4]

People like you and me, not big shots—just ordinary people—can accomplish amazing things if we work together as a team. Just like the American homesteaders learned years ago, we can make it if we work side by side. Will you commit yourself to contribute whatever you can to the team effort of making disciples?

NOTES

1. Bruce Larson, *There's A Lot More To Health Than Not Being Sick* (Waco, Texas: Word Books, 1981), 59–60.

2. John MacArthur, Jr., *The Ultimate Priority* (Chicago: Moody Press, 1983), 106.

3. Billy Graham, *The Holy Spirit* (Waco, Texas: Word Books, 1978), 72.

4. Peter Marshall, *Mr. Jones, Meet The Master* (New York: Fleming H. Revell, 1949), 57–58.

C H A P T E R   T E N
Involving the Church

W hat is the church's role in disciple-making? How does the church assist a Christian in reaching out to friends? I believe it is nearly impossible to make disciples without the help and leadership of the church.

George Gallup of the Princeton Religious Survey Institute made this disclosure recently: "Half of the unchurched feel organized religion is ineffective in helping people find meaning in life—and 39 percent of those going to church agree."[1] My own denomination, the Presbyterian Church U.S.A., needs to improve in disciple-making as much as anyone. Between 1968 and 1985 we lost, 1.1 million members in our denomination. In seventeen years one of every four Presbyterians left our church. *U.S. News and World Report* listed us as the percentage leader of the losers among the top ten Protestant denominations. Clearly, what we have been doing has not been working. Though some churches may not be faring well, the church is still at the center of God's plan to reach the world with the Gospel.

Why Disciple-Makers Need the Church
Down through the centuries God has used the church as His instrument for making disciples. Christians need the support of the church if they are to be effective in making disciples. I

want to ask two questions: (1) Why do Christians need the church to help them make disciples? and (2) How can the church help individual believers make disciples?

There are three answers. First, *Christ calls His people to make disciples, not converts.* In Matthew 28:19 Jesus says, "Therefore go make disciples of all nations." Notice our call is to make disciples, not converts. In fact, you will look in vain through the New Testament for the word convert. The word "Christian" is only used three times in the New Testament. In contrast, there are 266 references to the word "disciple."

"Disciple" has greater breadth of meaning than either "convert" or "Christian." To be a convert or Christian can mean little more than a verbal commitment of belief in Christ or an intellectual assent to Christ's divinity. A disciple implies someone committed to following and learning. It signifies an ongoing dedication to Christ. Once we understand that we're not called to seek converts but to make disciples, we quickly realize we need the church to give new believers the lifelong nurture in Christ they need.

Second, *Christ's church is God's chosen instrument for making disciples.* The church is both God's means and ends of discipleship. Ephesians 4:11-12 says, "It was He who gave some to be apostles, some to be prophets, some to be evangelists, some to be pastors and teachers to prepare God's people for works of service, so that the body of Christ may be built up." God wants His church to be built up. The church's task is to train and equip men and women in reaching people for Christ. Paul adds in verse 16, "From Him the whole body joined and held together by every supporting ligament grows and builds itself up in love." When all members are using their spiritual gifts properly, the body grows. God wants His church to grow. He wants us to reach people with the Gospel.

In Matthew we read Peter's well known confession before the Lord, "You are the Christ, the Son of the living God" (Matt. 16:16). Jesus replies to Peter, "And I tell you that you are Peter, and on this rock I will build my church and the gates of Hades will not overcome it. I will give you the keys to the kingdom of heaven. Whatever you bind on earth will be bound in Heaven, and whatever you loose on earth will be loosed in heaven" (Matt. 16:18-19). Built on the solid-rock foundation of Jesus Christ the church has the authority to forgive sins. Though some days we may wonder otherwise, Christ assures you and me the church will prevail, even to the gates of hell. Christ says, "I will build My church." It is His instrument for making disciples.

A third reason Christians need the church to help them make disciples is because *disciple-making is most effective when the church is at the center of the process*. People who come to Christ outside of the church generally do not see the church as significant to their continued spiritual growth. As a result, they will be less inclined to get involved in the church. *Time* did an interview with Win Arn, the director of the American Institute of Church Growth. They concluded: "The only reliable measure of any evangelistic crusade's success is the number of people who become 'responsible church members.' In 1976 a Billy Graham Crusade drew 434,100 people to Seattle's Kingdome in eight days, and 18,000 people 'came forward' to profess faith in Christ. Arn's survey, done a year later and just released, reveals that of these, 54 percent were people simply rededicating themselves in the faith. Local churches received 8,400 cards signed by converts. According to Arn's study, only 1,285 of these—about 15 percent—ended up as active church members. Graham's results, moreover, are far better than those of Bill Bright's much ballyhooed 'Here's Life, America' campaign. In a study of Indianapolis and Fresno, Arn's institute found that only a dismal 3 percent of the people who made 'decisions to accept Christ' over the telephone joined a church."[2]

On the other hand, if you came to Christ in the church, you're likely to see it as the place which will help you grow in

Christ. Most modern day evangelism is analogous to foster parenting. One person leads someone to Christ, then tries to give that new believer to a church that played no role in the person's coming to Christ. Since people are more inclined to seek nurture in a church if that local body was instrumental in their conversion, the church should make sure it is at the forefront of the process of leading men and women to Christ.

The Church: God's Instrument for Disciple-Making

Why does God consider the local church the best organism for making disciples? There are at least four reasons. First, *the church provides growth for all ages.* Most organizations outside the church cater to people in a particular age or interest group. But the church provides something for all ages, from toddlers to great-grandmothers.

The church also creates an environment which can provide people with spiritual and theological balance. Since the church gathers people of all ages from a variety of educational, socio-economic, and cultural backgrounds, these members come with diverse needs, concerns, and perspectives. Different viewpoints create a healthy tension that engenders Christian balance. If everyone in the church were alike we would be unbalanced in our understanding of Christ and Christian values. Diversity is healthy in the church.

Another way the church proves itself the best instrument for making disciples is by *providing people with a place and opportunity to worship.* The Bible makes it clear that worship is not primarily an individual pursuit, but a group action. We come to church to worship with other people who are seeking to worship the God of the universe. Though we can worship God while we are alone, God commands us not to forsake the assembling of ourselves together with other believers (Heb. 10:25). What better place can we find to worship with other Christians than in church?

Prior to becoming pastor of Sunset Presbyterian Church, I

served as a youth minister for eleven years. I developed a theory that the number one measure of spiritual growth in youth is their worship attendance. I observed, in nine out of ten cases, that when youth were regular in their church attendance, they were growing in Christ. When they were missing from worship or the youth group programs, the absences usually indicated a spiritual nosedive.

Merton Strommen in his book, *Five Cries of Youth,* cites a study which substantiates my theory. "In a complex computer analysis, thirty-nine possible predictors are analyzed simultaneously to determine what variables are most highly associated with saying 'My faith is important.' Our analysis shows that the most powerful predictor of youth who see faith as 'very important' is participation in the life of a congregation. Contrariwise, the most powerful indicator of youth for whom faith is not important is little or no participation in the life of their congregation."[3]

I believe what is true of youth is true of adults. When people drop out of regular worship attendance, it usually signals spiritual growth has stopped. Since worship is important to helping a Christian grow, churches need to monitor their worship attendance. Church leaders need to know who is coming and who is missing. Membership records need to be up to date and accurate. People need to be educated about the relationship of worship attendance to their spiritual development.

Everyone has heard excuses for why some people do not attend church regularly. Some of the best (or worst) excuses were put into print by a man who sent his pastor this letter:

Dear Pastor:

You often stress attendance at worship, Sunday School, and Bible study as being very important for a Christian, but I think a person ought to be excused for the following reasons and the number of times indicated:

Christmas (the Sundays before and after)	2 Sundays
July 4th (nobody ever stays home)	1 Sunday
Labor Day (got to get out of town)	1 Sunday
Memorial Day (got to visit my home)	1 Sunday
School Closing (the children really need a break)	1 Sunday
School Opens (one last trip)	1 Sunday
Family Reunions (two per family)	4 Sundays
Sleep Later (due to long and crazy Saturday night)	6 Sundays
Vacations and Long Weekends	6 Sundays
Bad Weather (rain, wind, fog, clouds, hot weather)	6 Sundays
Ballgames	4 Sundays
Unexpected Company (can't just leave)	5 Sundays
Time Changes (spring ahead, fall back)	2 Sundays
Specials on TV (Superbowl, etc.)	4 Sundays
Sickness	6 Sundays

Pastor, that only leaves two Sundays per year, so you can count on us to be there the third Sunday of March and the first Sunday in August. We look forward to seeing you then.

Sincerely,

E.X. Keuses[4]

Church leaders who recognize the importance of corporate worship to Christian growth plan worship services carefully. Christians who want to grow in Christ place a priority on worship and make church an important element in their lives.

Finally, the church is God's instrument *by providing both pastoral care for believers and outreach for nonbelievers.* The church must blend the ministries of pastoral care and evangelism. But here's the rub: Most Christian leaders make a sharp distinction between pastoral work and evangelism. They are considered two separate ministries. I agree that it is difficult for churches to do both well. Yet to separate these complementary ministries is unwise. The church must do both; people need to minister and to be ministered to.

Helping Believers Make Disciples

Once we are convinced that the church is God's best tool for disciple-making, we are ready to ask: How can a church help its members make disciples? There are several key elements.

First, *the pastoral staff must set an example of making disciples*. In Ezekiel we read of a condemnation against the pastoral shepherds of Israel:

> Woe to the shepherds of Israel who only take care of themselves! Should not shepherds take care of the flock? You eat the curds, clothe yourselves with the wool and slaughter the choice animals, but you do not take care of the flock. You have not strengthened the weak, or healed the sick or bound up the injured. You have not brought back the strays or searched for the lost. You have ruled them harshly and brutally. So they were scattered because there was no shepherd, and when they were scattered they became food for all the wild animals. My sheep wandered over all the mountains and on every high hill. They were scattered over the whole earth and no one searched or looked for them (Ezek. 34:2-6).

The pastoral shepherds of Israel were condemned for not searching for the lost. They allowed the members to scatter and never bothered to look for them or bring them back. Pastors must attempt to restore members who have wandered from Christ's body and seek out God's children who have never found the church. Shepherds should heal the hurts of people, not simply wait for people to come to them. Pastors are to be involved in evangelism, reaching out to the un-churched who don't know Christ, as well as pastoring the congregation.

Jesus said, "I am the Good Shepherd. The Good Shepherd lays down His life for the sheep" (John 10:11). He set the example. Jesus also tells a parable which shows the kind of pastor He is: "If a man owns a hundred sheep and one of them wanders away, will he not leave the ninety-nine on the hills and go to look for the one that wandered off? And if he finds it, I tell you the truth, he is happier about that one sheep than about the ninety-nine that did not wander off" (Matt. 18:12-13). Jesus' priority is the lost one. If today's pastors are to follow Christ's example they must be concerned about the lost, the unchurched, and the people who have left the church.

In 2 Timothy Paul instructs Timothy with these words: "Do the work of an evangelist. Discharge all the duties of your ministry" (4:5). In the Greek there is no definite article before the Greek word *euanggelistou*, which we translate 'evangelist'. This means that evangelism is not being assigned to Timothy as an additional job, but that outreach to unbelievers is part and parcel of his duty as a pastor. Paul is saying that the work of a pastor is to be concerned about the lost. Pastors need to blend the ministries of pastoring the churched and reaching out to the unchurched.

Jesus tells us, "A student is not above his teacher, but everyone who is fully trained will be like his teacher" (Luke 6:40). Students become like their teachers. Most of what we teach comes through modeling. If pastors want churches concerned with reaching unbelievers, they will have to set the example.

Any time our church sponsors an event that focuses on reaching out to nonbelievers, I make sure I bring a guest. I ask all of our pastoral staff to do the same. We can't expect our people to do anything we are not willing to do ourselves.

Caring for church members is a full-time job. So any time a

pastor commits to also reaching out to the unchurched, tension will be experienced. It's hard to do both. I know of one pastor who got a phone call one evening from a man who was sick and dying in a hospital across town. The man was not a Christian. He was a person who had been critical of the church for years, but he wanted a visit from the pastor. A minute later the minister received another phone call from a man who was an elder in the church. He also was on his death bed in a different hospital on the opposite side of town. Both were asking the reverend to come. If you were the pastor, which man would you visit first?

He prayed about it, then went to see the sick man who was not a Christian. The pastor's thought process went something like this: Though the elder is very important to me and I need to see him, at least he knows the Lord. He'll be with the Lord if he dies right now; the other man will not. As it turned out, the man he went to see became a Christian before he died. The elder recovered from his surgery, then left the church. He and his family were furious that the pastor did not come immediately to see him.

I'm not suggesting pastors ignore their congregations. Pastoral care is an important part of a minister's work. Pastors must see that their church members' needs are met. Members have a right to expect good care. The desire for loving oversight is one of the reasons they came to church. At the same time we must understand that Christ called pastors to also be concerned about the lost who are outside the church. Churches need to allow their pastors to minister both ways.

There's a second way the church can help its people to make disciples. *The church must have vision that puts a priority on disciple-making.* The church needs to state unequivocally that it is in the business of making disciples. Then the church must have a clear plan of how to go about reaching people for Christ. A church with purpose is a church that is alive. People come with anticipation every Sunday morning. They expect

God to do something in each worship service. People expect to experience the power of Christ in "their" ministry. They express their faith that God is going to do great things in their midst through visionary planning. They plan with faith. When they build a sanctuary they build one larger than the present membership, because they believe God will bring new people to Christ through their ministry. They build more and larger classrooms than they currently can utilize. They create more parking spaces than they need because they expect God will fill the spaces. They hire staff before there is an imminent need, so the church body can continue to expand. They recruit leaders first, and then expect programs to grow around these leaders. They plan ahead with the expectation that God blesses courageous faith.

Third, *the church must train people to make disciples.* Church leaders are to train the people of God for ministry. The goal of every church ought to be the mobilization of every member into some disciple-making role. The pastor must set an example, but this does not mean he does all the work of evangelism. Often the pastor's time is better spent training other people to make disciples.

During my years of ministry I have received a number of phone calls where someone says: "Ron, could you come help me? I'm going to talk with a friend who I think is ready to accept Christ. Would you lead him to the Lord for me?" My initial response is "Sure, I'll be right over." But by the time I get my keys, I begin to wonder if I'm doing the right thing. Instead of rushing over, I call the person on the phone and say, "Hey, I've been thinking. Why don't we talk about some questions you might ask, the answers you might give, and how you can lead your friend to Christ. You pray with your friend and lead him to the Lord. Why should I come over, take the hero role, and cheat you out of the privilege of leading your friend or family member to Christ? You are every bit as much a minister as I am."

The next time I see the caller, he or she has a big smile. They're delighted they had the privilege of leading their dad to the Lord, or helping a friend come closer to making a decision about Christ. This may have been the first time they've shared the Gospel with someone.

Fourth, *the worship service must assist people in making disciples.* When a worship service includes inspirational music, well-prepared sermons, people exhibiting genuine love, and the singing of praises to the Lord, worship can have a tremendous evangelistic appeal. Many people share that their first stirrings of the Holy Spirit came in a worship service where they sensed that there was something different about the people. There's no excuse for a worship service that's dull and lifeless.

Worship should be inspirational and planned with the visitor in mind. Members are more likely to invite friends if such an atmosphere is present.

Fifth, *the Sunday School must assist people in making disciples.* The Sunday School can aid in making disciples if its stated purpose is to help church members reach out. When churches organize Sunday School classes, they need to have disciple-making in mind. They need to ask what kind of topics we can offer that will encourage class members to invite neighbors and friends. What topics will meet the needs of people in this community? Regular class socials should be scheduled which encourage class members to invite friends.

If a church wants its Sunday School to help in the task of making disciples, it must begin new Sunday School classes each year. A typical Sunday School class will only assimilate new people for about eighteen months. When a new class begins people get acquainted and establish new friendships. After a few months of studying, working, and socializing together, people develop a camaraderie. As their relationships with fellow class members become more meaningful, their friendship circle closes. Their need for new friendships decreases. Without even realizing it, their class becomes less and less effective in assimilating new people. Visitors may try the class, but most will eventually drop out as they discover they are unable to break into the inner circle of fellowship. Churches should encourage the development of close friendships. But as they are successful in creating these social bonds, they must also create new classes to give new church members a chance to form lasting friendships.

Finally, *small caring groups must be structured to aid people in their efforts to make disciples.* Churches are most successful in making disciples if they make it clear that people can invite friends or neighbors to their caring groups. Small Bible study and prayer groups should be encouraged to multiply in number and divide. These warm, loving fellowship groups which usually meet in homes, can reach out to many new people, if they are designed with an "open membership." If groups become closed to new members, people are discouraged from inviting their friends.

Churches that want their small groups to reach new people will choose topics that will appeal to potential disciples. Many subjects can be of interest to people who have no church home. You might go to a neighbor and say, "You know, a lot of marriages today are really in trouble. We're having a study in our home where we'll look at what the Bible says about marriage. We'd love to have you join in the discussion." Many people feel a need to strengthen their marriage, and might take you up on your offer. Or you might say, "You know, the Bible is the number one selling book in the world. Yet we find most people have never read it. We're having a study in our home where we're going to look at the Gospel of Luke. We'd love to have you. Would you like to join us?" When invited by a close friend, you'd be surprised how many people respond positively to such an invitation.

We have forty caring groups in our church at the present time, each with ten to fifteen members. If each group would add one family to the church this next year, and each family averaged two to three members, that would be 100 new people brought to Christ. Small groups are a natural way for a church to reach out and make disciples. Unfortunately, the majority of study and fellowship groups in most churches never consider inviting neighbors or work associates. As a result, the groups quickly become ingrown and make no contribution to the church's mission. Instead, people focus their attention on one another and soon have no time or inclination to be concerned about others.

The church is essential in making disciples. Churches help by focusing on disciple-making in their church programming. Worship services, Sunday School classes, small groups, music ministries, and youth activities can contribute to the church's mandate.

Most of all, churches need to be loving. When church members bring visitors, they need to see people who love each other, who love God, and who notice and care for visitors. People want a place where they feel cared for, healed, and nurtured.

If, with God's help, we can create loving churches, members will want to bring their friends. Churches that care attract visitors. Churches that cultivate love and open their arms to new people are churches that grow.

NOTES

1. George Gallup, *Search for America's Faith* (Nashville: Abingdon Press, 1980), 153.

2. "Soul Saving—What Is the Bottom Line?" *Time,* 23 January 1978, 78.

3. Merton Strommen, *Five Cries of Youth* (New York: Harper & Row, 1974), 98–99.

4. Good Shepherd Assembly of God Newsletter, Carlsbad, California, August 1986.

CHAPTER ELEVEN
Parenting Children Wisely

March 30, 1981 brought fear into the hearts of most Americans. For hours we searched the dials on our radios and turned the channels on our televisions for the latest report on the condition of our president. That was the day John Hinckley, Jr. tried to assassinate President Ronald Reagan.

Nearly a year later, our nation was following Hinckley's trial. For many parents, one image of the Hinckley trial is indelible—John W. Hinckley, Sr., weeping on the stand in the Washington courtroom, taking responsibility for the gunshots fired by his twenty-six-year-old son at President Reagan. That moment of anguish summons a basic fear among other embattled parents: the fear that nothing will straighten out a problem son or daughter, not money, status, psychiatry, permissiveness, or even the H-bomb of the parent-child wars—tossing the troublemaker out of the house.

It's a tough world in which to raise kids. Many parents are in trouble and they know it. The cry of bewildered parents is heard around the world, "What can I do to help my child turn out 'right?' " Even Christian parents are frequently perplexed as to how to best raise their kids. I find that most parents are willing to try any method to help their child.

What concerns me is that I find so many parents ignoring

the most important priority in their attempts to help their children turn out "right." They fail to help their child become a disciple of Jesus Christ.

Parental Priorities

The top priority for many parents is to give their child the best possible *health*. They take the utmost care during pregnancy. Once born, the baby gets the best possible food and vitamins and adequate exercise. They make certain their child receives the best in medical care. As the years go by there will be many trips to dentists, orthodontists, opthamalogists, allergists and the like. Any parent who does less would be considered negligent. But using Scripture as my guide, this would not be my nomination for the most important priority of a parent.

Some parents would suggest that *education* is the top priority for the child. These parents buy as many stimulating and educational toys for their children as they can afford. They read scores of books to their children. As soon as "Junior" is old enough to read, the parent goes to the library with him each week to check out the maximum number of books. That youngster will inevitably be enrolled in numerous educational classes. If public schools are found to be inadequate, she will be sent to a private school. Yet, as important as it may be, education would not be my choice for the most important parental priority.

Other parents suggest, by their behavior, that the most important role of the parent is to help the child with *skill development*. These parents see to it that their children take lessons in art or music, or are involved in dance, ballet, karate, or judo. They send their athletic hopefuls to football, basketball, soccer or baseball camps, and provide them with tennis, swimming, or skiing lessons, etc. They are trying to help their sons and daughters develop skills in a certain area. But once again, this is not an area of ultimate priority for a parent.

Other parents seem to believe the most important task is to provide his or her child with *prosperity*. Long hours at work by one or both parents and numerous working weekends are rationalized as necessary for the future material well-being of the child. Family time is sacrificed again and again for the sake of career.

What then should the most important parental priority be? Scripture teaches that the number one priority for every parent is to help his or her child become a disciple of Jesus Christ. Jesus says, "What good is it for a man to gain the whole world, yet forfeit his soul? Or what can a man give in exchange for his soul?" (Mark 8:36-37) Jesus is saying to parents, what would it matter if your son becomes the star of the Boston Celtics, or your daughter is voted Miss America, or your child ranks number one in the graduating class from Harvard if, in the process, he loses his soul and never establishes a relationship with his Creator? Giving your child good health, the best education, well-developed talents, and monetary security are gifts of kindness, but they pale in importance with leading them into a relationship with Jesus Christ.

Revolutionary war hero Patrick Henry wrote at the conclusion of his last will and testament: "I have now disposed of all my property to my family. There is one thing more that I wish I could give them and that is faith in Jesus Christ. If they had that and I had not given them one shilling, they would have been rich; and if they had not that, and I had given them all the world, they would be poor indeed."[1]

We can liken this priority task of a parent to a relay race in a track meet. I used to run track in high school. I can assure you that most relay races are won or lost in the passing of the baton. I have never seen a runner drop the baton on the back side of the track when the baton is clasped tightly in his hand. If failure is to occur, it takes place in the transmission from one person to the next.

Picture yourself, Christian parent, as the runner. Your most important priority is to get the baton—the Gospel—into the hands of your child. You will want to place the Gospel in many other hands as well, but your foremost responsibility is to disciple your own children. No worldly success can compensate for failure in this strategic area of the home. To lead your own children to Christ is wise parenting.

Important as it is in parenting, I am sad to report to you that relatively little is written about the subject of leading your child to Christ. I have at least fifty books in my library about parenting, yet there is next to nothing in them about this top-priority task.

I am also amazed at the number of Christian parents I meet who spend hours developing their children's skills, yet fail to take the same care to insure that their children become disciples of Jesus Christ.

Thus far, we have considered seven elements in a strategy for making disciples. We have seen that most people come to Christ through the influence of a friend or family member. Since the majority of Christians credit a parent as the one who first pointed them to Christ, a strategy for making disciples would be incomplete without a word to parents about their important role. If all Christian parents were successful in making disciples of their own children, and saw to it that their children join in the call to make disciples of others, we would be well on our way toward reaching the world for Christ. I believe helping parents make disciples of their children should be the church's single greatest strategy for spreading the news of Jesus Christ.

Wise parents will do all they can to see that their children become disciples of Jesus Christ. It is one of the greatest commitments parents can make. What can a parent do to increase the likelihood of his or her child becoming a lifelong disciple of Jesus Christ? There are no fail-safe methods, but let me offer two suggestions that will help every parent encourage his or her child to follow Jesus Christ.

Lead Your Child to Christ

Wise parents lead their children to Christ. See to it your child has every opportunity to begin a relationship with the Lord Jesus. Concerning this challenge, two observations are crucial.

One is that *wise parents recognize Christian commitment does not come automatically.* Just because you are a Christian is no guarantee that your child will choose to follow Christ. The fact that I am a pastor is no assurance that my children will serve the Lord.

Scripture offers plenty of examples of God-fearing parents who did not raise faithful offspring. The book of 1 Samuel introduces us to Eli, a priest over Israel in the day of the judges, who was deeply committed to the Lord: "Eli's sons were wicked men; they had no regard for the Lord" (1 Sam. 2:12). Strange, isn't it, that the spiritual leader of the country was not able to convince his sons to follow the Lord?

Eli was followed by Samuel who became the prophet of the Lord to Israel. All Israel looked to Samuel when it needed wisdom or guidance, for he was the spokesman of the Lord. Yet in 1 Samuel 8:1-3, we find a disheartening disclosure: "When Samuel grew old, he appointed his sons as judges for Israel. The name of his firstborn was Joel and the name of his second was Abijah, and they served at Beersheba. But his sons did not walk in his ways. They turned aside after dishonest gain and accepted bribes and perverted justice." How was it that another respected prophet could wield such power in Israel, yet lose his own sons?

Years later, after Israel had become a divided kingdom with ten tribes of Israel in the north and Judah in the south, Jehoshaphat ascended the throne of Judah. He was a man who did what was right in the sight of the Lord. He obeyed God and led all of Judah to worship God alone. We are impressed by the impact he had for God, until we come to 2 Chronicles 21:1, 3-6. We read, "Then Jehoshaphat rested with his fathers and was buried with them in the City of David. And Jehoram his son succeeded him as king. Their father Jehoshaphat had given them [Jehoram's brothers] many gifts of silver and gold and articles of value, as well as fortified cities in Judah, but he had given the kingdom to Jehoram because he was his firstborn son. When Jehoram established himself firmly over his father's kingdom he put all his brothers to the sword along with some of the princes of Israel. Jehoram was thirty-two years old when he became king, and he reigned in Jerusalem eight years. He walked in the ways of the kings of Israel, as the house of Ahab had done for he married a daughter of Ahab. He did evil in the eyes of the Lord." How could Jehoshaphat lead all of Judah to obey God, yet not win his own son?

Several generations later, Hezekiah assumed his reign as king over Judah. He led a great revival. Altars to false gods were torn down all over the country. Then, in 2 Kings 20:21–21:2, we read these sobering words, "Hezekiah rested with his fathers. And Manasseh his son succeeded him as king. Manasseh was twelve years old when he became king, and he reigned in Jerusalem fifty-five years. His mother's name was Hephzibah. He did evil in the eyes of the Lord, following the detestable practices of the nations the Lord had driven out before the Israelites." How could it be that he could lead a revival throughout his country, yet never reach his son spiritually?

Decades later, Josiah led another revival in Judah. He was one of the most godly and obedient kings in the history of Judah. But once again we are disappointed. We read of his son in 2 Chronicles 36:5, "Jehoiakim was twenty-five years old when he became king, and he reigned in Jerusalem eleven years. He did evil in the eyes of the Lord his God." We are left wondering how a revivalist could not even bring revival into his own family.

We could go on and on with many other examples. Where did David go wrong with Absalom? How did Solomon fail in communicating his wisdom and love for the Lord to Rehoboam? It is clear that commitment to the Lord is not automatically transmitted from parents to children.

Let me add a word in defense of these biblical parents and all parents. Scripture teaches that God loves all people and desires all men and women to come to faith in Christ. Yet, we are also taught that God has created man with freedom of choice. Although He wants all to come to salvation, some choose to reject Him. If God can be rejected, we certainly must accept that the faith and good intentions of a parent can be rejected. If you are a parent of a son or daughter who is not following the Lord, you need not take full responsibility for the choices of your son or daughter. Children can reject the faith of their parents, and many times do.

Knowing that faith is not automatically transferred from one generation to the next ought to cause parents to redouble their efforts to lead their children to Christ. Statistics suggest that most fathers spend less than one mintue a day in meaningful conversation with their children and that the average young child watches thirty to fifty hours of television each week.[2] With such forces working on our children, we can be sure they will not automatically come to share our values—especially our Christian faith. Unless we make a concerted effort to bring our children to Christ, the odds are decidedly against their sharing our faith.

My second observation is that *wise parents offer their children an opportunity to respond to Christ at an early age.* In Mark 10:13-16, we read, "People were bringing little children to Jesus to have Him touch them, but the disciples rebuked them. When Jesus saw this He was indignant. He said to them, 'Let the little children come to Me, and do not hinder them, for the kingdom of God belongs to such as these. I tell you the truth, anyone who will not receive the kingdom of God like a little child will never enter it.' And He took the children in His arms, put His hands on them and blessed them.'" We cannot be certain of the exact ages of the children who were brought to Jesus, but the Greek word, *paidia,* which is translated, "little children," refers to children or infants.

I believe we have the same problem today that the disciples had centuries ago. They were indignant that people were bringing children to Jesus. They figured that Jesus was too busy for children. Similar opinions circulate today. There are people who insist that children should not be in Sunday worship. Some people believe that preschool children are too young to make commitments to Christ. I have visited and heard of churches and Vacation Bible Schools that do not offer programs for children younger than five years of age. Yet, Jesus' answer to His disciples seems to clearly communicate that there is no age at which a child is too young to be brought to Jesus.

Dr. Benjamin Bloom, of the University of Chicago, has summarized an immense number of research studies which demonstrate the startling fact that a child develops approximately 50 percent of his intelligence by the age of four, another 30 percent by the age of eight, and the remaining 20 percent by the age of seventeen.[3]

If a child develops 50 percent of his intelligence by the age of four, I strongly believe that child is capable of responding to the Spirit of God. And if a child develops 80 percent of his intelligence by the age of eight, we are deluding ourselves if we think such a youngster is too young to make an intelligent decision about Jesus Christ.

I am suggesting that parents shouldn't refrain from sharing the claims of Christ with their children because they feel they are too young. Provide your children with an opportunity to invite Christ into their lives. They'll let you know if they do not yet understand or are not ready. But let them make that decision. Don't make that assumption for them.

Some of you may object, "When you seek to evangelize children at such early ages, aren't you taking advantage of vulnerable, impressionable, and defenseless people?" That, of course, is a danger, but it is not what I am suggesting. If you ask your child if he would like to thank Jesus for dying for his sins, confess his sins, and invite Jesus into his life, you must make sure that it is his or her decision and not yours.

Still, you may object, "Since it is the Holy Spirit's role to draw people to Christ, aren't parents displacing the role of the Holy Spirit if they invite their children to make a commitment to Christ?" Not at all. No one can come to Christ unless the Holy Spirit draws him. But that truth in no way denies human agency in the process of salvation. In fact, except for rare exceptions, God seldom draws anyone to Himself apart from involvement by loving disciplers. The truth is you may well be the agent, under the guidance of the Holy Spirit, upon whom God is relying to lead your child to Christ.

Share in the joy. Talk to your child about the love of Jesus Christ. Remember, wise parents seek to offer their children an opportunity to respond to Christ's call at an early age. Wise parents lead their children to Christ.

Lead Your Child Into Disciple-Making

My second suggestion to help parents see their children become disciples is this: *Wise parents help their children become involved in the process of making disciples.* A Christian parent's task is not completed when his son or daughter makes a commitment to Christ. Jesus did not call us to make "Christians," but to make "disciples." Once our child comes to Christ, we need to do all we can to cause him or her to grow in Christ.

What can we do to spur our child on to maturity in Christ? There are many things we can do. But I know of nothing that spurs growth faster than encouraging your son or daughter to be involved in the disciple-making process. Unless your children see the importance of making disciples, they may not really understand the Christian message or be growing in their relationship with Christ. Remember, Christians grow mature in Christ as they serve, minister, and share Christ's love with others. The Apostle Paul instructs Timothy with these words, "And the things you have heard me say in the presence of many witnesses entrust to reliable men who will also be qualified to teach others" (2 Tim. 2:2). We are called to entrust the Gospel to people who are able to pass it on to others. The goal is the same for our children. We must do more than give them the Gospel; we must also encourage and enable them to pass it on to others.

In the bluegrass country of Kentucky you will find many retired, champion race horses that are now being used to father other horses. Stud fees from a champion horse run from $2,000 to $3,000. But once the champion has sired an offspring who wins the Derby, the stud fee goes up to $40,000 to $50,000. The most valuable horse is not one who wins himself, but the one who sires a winner. The greatest contribution you can make is not just in bringing your child to Christ, but in helping your child become a disciple-maker.

Once again, I encourage you to involve your son or daughter in the task of making disciples at as early an age as possible. Don't make the mistake of assuming that a person cannot point others to the Saviour until he reaches adulthood. Young people can have a great impact for God in their teenage and even their grade-school years.

One of the best biblical examples of this truth is found in 2 Chronicles 34:1-2: "Josiah was eight years old when he became king, and reigned in Jerusalem thirty-one years. He did what was right in the eyes of the Lord and walked in the ways of his father David, not turning aside to the right or to the left." At eight years old he was already committed to the Lord and leading his country in the path of following God. Again, in verse 3, we read, "In the eighth year of his reign, while he was still young, he began to seek the God of his father David. In his twelfth year he began to purge Judah and Jerusalem of high places, Asherah poles, carved idols and cast images." That means that between the age of sixteen and twenty he led a major revival in Judah. Young people who give their lives to Christ can make a significant difference in this world and can fill a significant role in the church's task of making disciples.

Disciple-Making Helps a Child Mature in Christ

How can an involvement in making disciples help your child grow toward maturity in Christ? I would like to mention three ways. First, *disciple-making helps children develop an eternal perspective.* They begin to see all people in light of an eternity with or without Christ. They realize that one's eternal destiny is an individual choice.

Second, *disciple-making helps children grow in their faith.* Reaching out to others strengthens us in our faith. Before we can share Christ with others, we must understand who Christ is and what it is we believe about Him. When we seek to make disciples we have to pray. If we are to have a message to share, we must be growing in Christ.

Third, *disciple-making helps children focus their attention on caring for others.* Nothing helps us grow quite as quickly as focusing on the needs of others rather than on ourselves. I received this letter from a young girl in our church.

Dear Pastor Ron,

If you have the time this week, please try to answer my letter. I'm going to take on a mission this week to try to bring a girl at my school to Christ. She's always making fun of others and putting others down. I can tell that she needs God in her life. Your sermon this last week has really made a difference in me. It has changed the way I live and especially the way I pray. I would like it a lot if you could give me some tips on this and pray for me as I take on this mission. It would really mean alot to me.

Love in Christ,

Joy Donahue

I see here a person who is growing in her faith because she is attending to the needs of someone else. There is no unhappier person than the person who is always concerned about self. She is growing because she is giving herself to the task of making a disciple. Wise is the parent who encourages his son or daughter to help others find Christ.

There's not a parent in this world that wants to have the courtroom experience of John W. Hinckley, Sr. We want our children to turn out "right." Toward that end, my counsel to you is twofold: lead your child to Christ, and help your child become involved in making disciples. One of the most important things you can do to spread the news of Christ in this world is to reach your child.

NOTES

1. Patrick Henry, *Book for Those in Positions of Responsibility* (Nashville: Thomas Nelson Inc., 1978), 46.

2. James Dobson, *Straight Talk to Men and Their Wives* (Waco, Texas: Word Books, 1980), 36.

3. Fitzhugh Dodson, *How to Parent* (Los Angeles: Nash Publishing, 1970), 28–29.

CHAPTER TWELVE
Sharing Your Faith

Communication is essential to living. But we often find communicating difficult. Whether our communication is nonverbal, spoken, or written, it is easy for our messages to be unclear. The story of a conversation between a Mexican immigrant who knew very little English and an American illustrates how difficult it can be to communicate. A Mexican came to a man's house one day, knocked on the door, and said he needed something to eat. The homeowner replied, "Fine, I'll give you something to eat, but I believe strongly in the work ethic. If you do some work for me, I'll give you something to eat." The needy man agreed. The owner told the man to go to the back yard where he would find a bucket of paint and a paintbrush. "Paint the porch and when you're done, come back and I'll give you some food."

The man was gone for two or three hours. Finally he came back, knocked on the front door and said, "Me finished, Señor." The man seemed pleased and said, "Great, come on in and I'll give you something to eat." The Mexican replied, "Before we eat I think you need to know you made a mistake about what you told me to paint. It wasn't a Porsche. It was a Mercedes!"

Obviously, clear communication is not a given. How do we communicate? A study done at Colgate University some years ago revealed that our personal communication comes through three means. Only 7 percent of our communication is verbal. That means if we are putting all our emphasis on verbal communication, we are fighting a losing battle. Thirty-eight percent of our messages come through our actions, while 55 percent of communication comes through our attitude.

We who want to communicate the Gospel need to remember these three elements in communication. Most of the Gospel is communicated through our attitudes. If we have an attitude of love toward other people, we will be good communicators of the news of Christ. If our actions bring honor to God, then we will be walking communicators of the Gospel. Though words are not our primary means of communicating with others, they too are essential if we hope to make clear the message of God's love for the world.

We saw in Chapter 1, four primary steps in the process of making disciples: cultivation, proclamation, instruction, and reproduction. When a person becomes a Christian, the third step in the process of disciple-making—instruction in the Scriptures—is needed to help that new believer grow toward maturity in Christ. If Christians are to continue to mature in Christ, they must get involved in the next step of the disciple-making process—spiritual reproduction. Christ calls all believers to reproduce their faith. Jesus' first instructions to His followers in Mark were, "Come, follow Me and I will make you fishers of men" (1:17). His last words to His disciples, recorded in Acts 1:8, were "You will be My witnesses in Jerusalem and in all Judea and Samaria, and to the ends of the earth." Christ began and ended His ministry with a command to evangelize. His command is for all Christians. The acid test of any church's evangelism program will ultimately be: Is it producing spiritual grandchildren and great-grandchildren? If not, something is amiss. If Christians do not reproduce themselves spiritually, then the whole process of making disciples breaks down. Churches will not grow.

When a Christian becomes involved in spiritual reproduction, the place to begin in communicating the Gospel is by cultivating relationships. When we cultivate relationships, we communicate primarily through our attitudes and actions. Through love, kind deeds, and a visible change in lifestyle we build relationships with people and communicate the Good News of Jesus Christ.

If the Gospel was communicated only through our attitudes and actions, however, it would be incomplete. What people see must be verbally interpreted before the communication circle is closed. Eventually we must come to the next step in the process of making disciples—proclamation. Words must be used to give the non-Christian a clear statement of the essential message of the Gospel—the underlying reason for our attitudes and actions.

Paul tells us the importance of "words" in proclaiming the Gospel: "How, then, can they call on the one they have not believed in? And how can they believe in the one of whom they have not heard? And how can they hear without someone preaching to them?" (Rom. 10:14) People cannot believe unless the Gospel is made clear to them—in words.

Peter understood the importance of words complementing attitudes and actions in his counsel to us: "But in your hearts set apart Christ as Lord. Always be prepared to give an answer to everyone who asks you to give the reason for the hope that you have" (1 Peter 3:15). He tells us that Christians must be prepared to speak the gospel. *An effective disciple-maker must know how to verbalize his faith.* I would like to look at the three elements necessary to communicate the Gospel, placing special emphasis on how we should verbalize our faith, by looking at Peter's counsel in 1 Peter 3:15-16.

Actions

To communicate the gospel effectively we must have *the right actions.* Peter says, "But in your hearts set apart Christ as

Lord." Christ must be Lord of our lives. To set apart the Lord in our hearts means to obey Him. We communicate right actions through *obedience*. First John 2:3-4 says, "We know that we have come to know Him if we obey His commands. The man who says 'I know Him,' but does not do what He commands is a liar, and the truth is not in him." When we obey Christ, we communicate a changed lifestyle that attracts people to Christ.

When we set apart Christ as Lord in our hearts we also exhibit the right actions of *love*. The natural result of loving Christ is to love our neighbor. John says, "Whoever does not love does not know God, because God is love" (1 John 4:8). When we love people, we are able to develop relationships of trust that become the basis for a spiritual bond.

Peter says, we must be ready "to give an answer to everyone." When we live a life of obedience and love, people will be curious to know what makes us different. People will come to us for counsel. They will ask us questions. Opportunities will arise to share our faith in Jesus Christ. We must be prepared for these opportunities.

We hold in the Gospel the only hope for people in this world. People desperately need to know about Jesus. They need us to share Him with them. When we communicate through right actions, we will have opportunities to share the reason for the hope that is in us, so we must be prepared to verbalize our faith.

Words

To communicate our faith effectively we must have *the right words*. Peter says, "Be prepared to give an answer to everyone who asks you." How can we be prepared to speak the right words?

First, *speak to the person's point of need*. Unless we speak to the needs of a person, we don't stand a chance of being heard. Every person has a built-in filter system. People filter out what they perceive to be irrelevant. If we are to communicate with people we must get through their filter system. Speak to the person's felt needs. Scratch people where they itch. A recent study has shown that over 80 percent of those who trust Christ and remain in fellowship with a local church were born again during a period of personal crisis.[1] Find out where people are hurting and speak to those hurts.

Anyone who has children has a felt need in the area of parenting. If you want to reach parents, meet the needs of their children. A study at the Princeton Religious Research Center found that in 1952 only 6 percent of Americans had had no religious training. In 1965, 9 percent said they had had no religious training. By 1978, 17 percent declared no religious training in their background. By 1981 an amazing 21 percent could claim no religious training. Ninety-five percent of unchurched people expressed a desire for their children to receive religious instruction. Fifty-two percent of the unchurched could imagine circumstances in which they would become active churchgoers.[2] We find that there is an increasing number of unchurched people who have had no religious instruction, who nevertheless, would like their children to receive some religious training. That means that any church that provides creative programs to meet the felt needs of children and their parents will find many unchurched people ready to respond. Our task is to discover these needs and speak to them at their point of need.

Second, *speak of the difference Christ has made in your life.* One of the most convincing arguments on earth regarding Christianity is one's personal experience with Jesus Christ. Know your own story. The steps that led to your conversion and subsequent ramifications are far more appealing to nonbelievers than a pulpit exposition of John 3 or Romans 3. No persuasive technique will ever take the place of your testimony. Write out your story. At our church membership classes, I ask each of our new members to write out the difference Christ has made in his or her life. They practice sharing their story with someone else in the class. This prepares them to share their faith when an opportunity arises. There are few forces in the world that can match the power of the personal testimony.

In Luke 8, Jesus casts demons out of a man from Gadara—a man who, under demonic control, could neither be clothed nor chained. Once delivered, however, the man sits clothed and in his right mind, listening hungrily to the words of Jesus. In sheer gratitude the Gadarene asks permission to accompany Jesus, but his request is denied. Instead, Jesus replies, "Return home and tell how much God has done for you" (v. 39). Then the text continues, "So the man went away and told all over town how much Jesus had done for him" (v. 40). Jesus knew that this man's personal testimony would be far more powerful in his home town than on the road with people who had never known his former existence.

When I say "personal testimony," I'm talking about a simple recital of what God has done for you and is doing in your life. You shouldn't need any techniques for telling about the changes Christ is making in your life. What excited explorer or research scientist needs techniques to communicate his discoveries? Talk about what you're learning. Share a recent answer to prayer. If you are growing in Christ, you should have some exciting stories to share.

I began dating Jorie about nine months after her first husband had died of cancer. He was a seminary student, so all the professors and students had been praying for his healing and for his young wife Jorie. But the Lord chose to take him home. I was a Young Life Club leader at the time. Several months after her husband's death Jorie joined our leadership team. Since it was not considered "kosher" for a Young Life leader to date members of his staff, and since everyone on the seminary campus knew about Jorie's tragic loss, we decided to do some undercover dating. We wanted to avoid a fishbowl relationship. After six months of fascinating, secretive dating we decided it was time to let people know we were dating. Let me tell you, when we went public I wanted everyone to know. Nobody had to tell me how to share my happy news. It came naturally.

In the same manner, the best way to verbalize your faith in Christ is to simply tell what Christ means to you. Share your excitement with what Christ is doing in your life or in your church.

Third, *speak about the Gospel of Jesus Christ.* We must know the Gospel message and be able to state it as simply as possible. Stated in as spare a fashion as possible, there are three essential tenets of the Christian faith.

Essential Tenets of the Faith
The first tenet is *Jesus Christ, the Son of God.* The Christian message is that Jesus Christ is the Son of God and creator of the world. As the Son of God, we recognize Him as the one we all must give an accounting to someday, for He will be everyone's final judge. As the Son of God, we recognize Him as God's final and fullest expression of Himself. To see Christ is to see God. To know Christ is to know God. To worship Christ is to worship God.

We learn about Christ from the Bible. This means that any Christian who hopes to share the Gospel must know the Bible. We must know passages of Scripture that tell who Christ is. Only if we know the Scriptures can we tell other people the content of God's Word. We need to challenge people to search the Scriptures. When I meet people who do not believe in Jesus Christ, nine out of ten times I discover that they have never read the Bible. Try asking them questions like, "Since you say that the evidence for Jesus Christ is terribly insufficient, where did you find the New Testament documents lacking?" In most cases you will find that the person has never read the Bible critically as an adult.

Another essential tenet of Christianity is *Jesus Christ, the*

Saviour. Jesus is not only the all-powerful and all-knowing God of the universe; He is also the Saviour. He is not a deistic God who is unknowable and uncaring. He came to planet earth as a man. Fully God and fully man, He died for us. He died for all our sins that make a barrier between us and God. He died to save us from our sins and to offer us forgiveness of sins. As Saviour, we realize not only that Christ created us, but that He also loves us and has come to bring us back into a relationship with Him.

A final essential tenet is *Jesus Christ, the Lord.* It is not enough to simply believe that Jesus Christ is the Son of God and Saviour of the world. Christianity is far more than a belief system. It is a relationship. Whenever we speak about the Gospel, our message should always lead the interested person toward an intimate encounter with Christ. No one becomes a Christian simply by believing that Jesus is God's Son and that He died on the cross for our sins. A person becomes a Christian when he claims Christ as Lord. Paul writes in Romans, "If you confess with your mouth, 'Jesus is Lord,' and believe in your heart that God raised Him from the dead, you will be saved" (10:9). We become Christians when we make the Lord our Lord. Salvation occurs when a person opens himself up to Christ and says, "What do you want me to do, Lord?"

Three elements of personality are involved in making a decision to become a Christian, or for that matter, in making any decision—the emotions, the intellect, and the will.

When I first met Jorie, if my emotions had their way, I would have gotten married that very night. I was leading a Young Life Club leaders' meeting. I had been told by the head Young Life staff woman that she was sending Jorie, a new potential leader, to our meeting. When she came up the stairs to the room where we were meeting, I saw this young lady with a dark tan and breathtaking long, blonde hair. I thought she was beautiful.

At the end of the meeting I had us close in prayer. I had all ten leaders sit in a circle on the floor. Then I had us join hands. Naturally, I positioned myself so I would be seated next to Jorie. Such planning! As we prayed—most of us sitting cross-legged—I let my knee touch hers. To this day, I don't remember a word of the prayers that night. All I can remember is her hand in mine and my romantic knee touching hers. Emotionally, I was already in love.

Then I had to get my intellect involved in the decision-making process. I had to get to know her. I had to decide if we were well-suited for each other.

Most importantly, I had to make a decision of the will, the third element in decision-making. I had to ask myself, "Am I ready to get married?" "Do I have the maturity and love this girl needs?" "Am I willing to commit 'to love and to cherish as long as we both shall live?'"

The will is man's greatest impediment to personal faith. Ever since the fall, man's basic problem has been rebellion against God. None of us are naturally willing to submit to God. To become a Christian, however, we must submit to God and make him Lord of our lives. When we speak about the Gospel, we are calling people to commit themselves to making Christ Lord of their lives.

Attitude

Peter tells us that to communicate the Gospel effectively we need the right actions, the right words, and finally, we need the *right attitude*. He writes, "But do this with gentleness and respect, keeping a clear conscience" (1 Peter 3:15-16). He mentions at least three qualities or types of attitude we need to have as we share the Gospel.

We need an attitude of *humility*. We must not come on as being better than the person with whom we are talking. I must see myself simply as one beggar telling another beggar where to find bread.

We also need an attitude of *respect*. We must respect the

other person's right to choose or reject the Gospel message. We must respect everyone's freedom of choice.

The Greek word we translate "respect," literally means "fear." When we share the Gospel we must respect the opinions of the one with whom we are speaking. I think this also means we must share the Gospel with a fear of or a respect for the power of God. We recognize that it is God, by the power of the Holy Spirit, who convicts people of sin and draws them to Himself. We must be patient and wait on the timing of the Holy Spirit. We must rely on the power of the Holy Spirit. No one comes to Christ apart from the power of the Holy Spirit. You will recall that Jesus told His disciples that they were to wait to share the message of His resurrection until after the Holy Spirit came. They could do nothing without the Holy Spirit. We must respect the Spirit's power and humbly recognize that we have no power of our own.

Peter also tells us we are to have an attitude of *purity*. We are to keep our conscience clear. Our life must match our words. We must obey Christ and keep our conscience clear so that we can declare that He really is making a difference in our lives.

The Challenge

To effectively communicate the Gospel, we need all three elements—right actions, words, and attitudes. Christ has called all believers to communicate His Gospel. Essential to that process, we must know how to verbalize our faith. We must be ready and willing to speak to people's point of need, speak of the difference Christ is making in our lives, and speak about the Gospel.

Reaching out to our neighbors is not an optional extra. Christ calls all Christians to make disciples. If we are to grow toward maturity we must give ourselves to making disciples. We cannot hope to grow in our faith unless we give ourselves to ministering in Christ's name. If we want our church to grow, we will have to reach out to people who do not know the Lord. Prayer, obedient living, love, cultivation of relationships, utilization of spiritual gifts, Christian teamwork, wise parenting, and sharing our faith all work together toward the end of helping men and women, and boys and girls meet Jesus Christ. The New Testament Church's preoccupation was with spreading the Good News about Jesus Christ. It must become, once again, the burning passion of every believer and church today.

Jeff West wrote this poignant story entitled *Your Neighbor* which, sad to say, is all too true.

You know me. I'm the fellow that takes care of your house when you go on vacation. Sometimes we cook out together on Saturday nights and the kids play in the yard. Our wives are good friends. They drink coffee together, trade recipes, and car pool the children. We talk together often about football and politics and inflation. We share a lot of the same ambitions and goals. Sometimes we share the same frustrations and disappointments. We are a lot alike—me and you. We're both good men. We want the best for our families. We determine to stand against adversity, to try, to persevere. We have ideals that we cling to just as a child clings to an outstretched hand. But sometimes you seem to have more strength than I have.

On Sunday morning I may be in the yard watering the grass and you drive by with your family—all of you dressed in your Sunday best—and you wave at me. And I wave back knowing where you are going but not why.

Sometimes it seems that your life is different from mine. Our wives have talked about it, but you and I are scared to mention it. There's a lot about you that I don't know. There's an emptiness in my life—a void that I just can't seem to fill, no matter how hard I try. It's not solved by the causal and infrequent invitation to revival or some special event. I need desperately to be answered, to be comforted, to know. And I need someone to tell me.

But we go on; and I don't mention it because some unknown fear prevents me, and you don't mention it because some unknown power binds you. We laugh together; we joke; we share, but not the important things. No, never the important things. Maybe someday. Maybe never.

I'm your neighbor, and I don't know Jesus.

Jesus told us "the harvest is plentiful." In other words, there are neighbors all around you and me who desperately need Christ and are ready to hear about Him. When will you share with your neighbor what Jesus means to you?

NOTES

1. Joseph C. Aldrich, "Unleashing Lifestyle Evangelism," *Global Church Growth*, no. 4 (Fall 1987): 8.

2. James E. Solheim, "The Unchurched Americans," *Presbyterian Survey*, April 1985, 16–17.

DATE DUE / DATE DE RETOUR

CARR McLEAN   38-297